Gr. 5 - 8

Confront
HISTORY
Simulations of Historical Conflicts

The Boston Tea Party
The Pequot War

The Fugitive Slave Law
The Alamo

Written by
Katie Collins
Illustrated by
Mary Lou Johnson

Dedication and Thanks

To Kirt . . . It all started with the Mexican War.

With special thanks to Mrs. Spark and her 5th grade students for their piloting the materials in this book

Edited by **Dianne Draze** and **Sonsie Conroy**

ISBN 1-883055-19-9

Table of Contents

Information for the Instructor

About This Book

Confronting History presents a unique opportunity for students to explore historical conflicts first-hand. Four different scenarios are presented, each one a conflict that involved people with differing viewpoints and motivations. By taking on the roles of some of the characters in these conflicts, students learn that in every situation there is more than one side.

In each simulation characters present their feelings, thus setting the stage for a discussion about the differing points of view and the dilemma these conflicting stands present. Students will see that people on each side of the conflicts felt that they had legitimate reasons for feeling and acting the way they did. They will see history not just as a series of events and dates but as situations that were interlaced with human emotions. They will come to understand that each conflict was a result of human feelings, needs, ambitions, and weaknesses. As students take on the historic characters, the human side of history will emerge.

After the many-faceted backdrop of each conflict has been presented, a group of students will work together to find a solution to the situation that will avoid conflict and will satisfy as many people as possible. At this point students will be deeply involved in history, debating the validity of each point of view, analyzing the many factors at play in the situation, creatively seeking a resolution, and evaluating the situation in relation to present-day conditions and events.

The four simulations in this book are:

. **The Pequot War** (1600 - 1671) - This unit shows the conflict not only between Native Americans and the European settlers, but also the conflicts among tribes that were created by the intrusion of white settlers.

. **The Boston Tea Party** (1763 - 1776) - This unit reenacts the tension between colonists in America and the English government when the English imposed taxes on their American subjects.

. **The Alamo** (1821 - 1836) - This conflict presents the clash between the interests of American settlers in Texas and the Mexican government.

The Fugitive Slave Law (1750 - 1850) - Presented mainly through the story of two run-away slaves, the conflict reflects larger issues that nearly tore the United States in two.

Hearing Procedures

Once an event has been chosen for study, follow the procedure described below to bring the historical conflict to life. Since the activities in this book are open-ended, it is up to the discretion and direction of the teacher to set time limits. The amount of student input through discussion and/or extended activities will allow each unit to extend over a four-day to three-week period. The following shows two possible time schedules. You may choose a schedule that falls somewhere between these two in the amount of time devoted to the project.

Four Day Plan - 50-90 minute sessions

Day 1 - Background information is read and discussed. Roles are assigned. Groups meet briefly. Additional preparation is done independently.

Day 2 - Groups meet, receive assignment sheets, and prepare for the hearing by acquainting themselves with the material and planning their questions.

Day 3 - The hearing takes place.

Day 4 - Resolution and closing statements are read. The Public Voice activities are presented.

Three Week Plan - 45-60 minute sessions

Week 1 - Background information is read and discussed thoroughly. Lists of research topics are distributed. Students work on research reports and present their information at the end of the week.

Week 2 - Background information is reviewed. Roles are discussed and chosen. Extension activities are chosen and students begin working on their activities.

Week 3 - The hearing takes place. Students portraying the Public Voice prepare a newscast or newspaper for the end of the week. Extension activities and discussion of the resolution complete the week.

■ Before You Start

1. Make individual folders for each student to store materials received during the activity.

2. The *Background Information* presented for each unit gives the basic information students need to understand the conflict, but the more information they have about the situation, the more realistic and compelling the situation will seem. For this reason, you will probably want to have your students do additional research. Collect reference material from your library. Make a list of people, places and things related to the incident that students can use for additional research.

3. Get a map that shows the area that will be studied.

4. Duplicate all materials that will be distributed to the students.

■ Getting Started

1. Distribute the *Background Information* sheets to all students.

2. Read and discuss the *Background Information* as if describing the prologue to a play.

3. Refer to the *Extension Activities* (pages 18-19) pages for suggested activities to encourage a greater awareness and understanding of the people and times surrounding each historical event. You can assign the research and extension activities for students who are not on the Mediator Team and will not be spending time seeking a resolution.

■ Assigning Roles

Introduce students to the Who's Who characters profiled on the *Meet the People* sheet. It is these people whose voices will be heard during the Crisis Hearing. All students will receive profiles of all the Who's Who characters. Next introduce and explain all the different roles the students will perform during the simulation.

Character Roles

Students choose (by explaining their reasons in a letter to you, by random choice, or some other method) or are appointed to one of the character roles described below. The roles are:

✳ **Mediator Team** - A panel of five, these students act as the listeners, evaluators, and problem-solvers for the historical hearing. The panel of five is broken down into three roles. They are:

Lead Mediator - One person chosen to direct and redirect the panel and historical figures during the hearing.

Recorder - One person chosen to keep an ongoing record during the hearing that may be useful in the final decision-making process.

Investigators - These three students stimulate discussion by asking questions of the Who's Who characters. Their goal should be to investigate and clarify the reasons these people feel the way they do.

Refer to the Mediator Team's job description on page 8 for a more detailed description of each role. Each Mediator Team member also receives a copy of each of the Diary Entries to be used as evidence in the hearing.

✳ **Who's Who** - Each historical incident has three to five students who choose or are appointed to represent each one of the historical figures for a total of nine to fifteen students representing the different perspectives. Who's Who members work in small groups, each group representing a different historical character. Each member in the group receives the diary entry for their historical figure. Refer to the Who's Who job description on page 9 for more detailed information.

✳ **Public Voice** - The other students in the class will fulfill one of the roles that represent the media and the public. These supportive roles are provided to create a more authentic and involved hearing. They are:

News Reporters - These people are responsible for summarizing the day's events for news updates. They are also encouraged to interview the historical figures before, during, and after the hearing. They can create their own newspaper, radio or television newscast. They can work together or independently of each other.

Photographers - These people are responsible for sharing the Crisis Hearing visually with the public. Actual pictures or videos can be taken or scenes of the hearing can be recreated through sketches or drawings and can then be used in newspaper or TV newscasts. Cartoons depicting the humorous or serious sides to the story are also possible. Captions should be developed for the photos, drawings and cartoons.

Bystanders - Their job is to watch and listen to the hearing with a somewhat sympathetic, yet curious ear. They are responsible for writing letters to the editor of the newspaper, radio or television newscasts, sharing their opinions on the situation or stances of the individual characters in the conflict.

■ Conducting the Hearing

The optimum seating arrangement is a circle, with the various groups sitting together, side by side. The circle promotes participation, acceptance, and discussion. Once students are seated, the procedure for carrying out the Crisis Hearing is:

1. Mediator Team leader invites each Who's Who team to make an opening statement for a predetermined amount of time. Opening statements are to be presented by the Who's Who spokesperson. The Diary Entry may be read or an informal summary may be shared.

2. After each group has been represented, the Investigators begin questioning the Who's Who teams using the questions devised specifically for this event. Team members may all have a chance to speak or can have the spokesperson convey their answers. Questioning should be fair and equal to all sides. Remind them that for every one side of the story, there is another side waiting to be heard.

3. The Public Voice members are to listen intently to what is being presented in order to improve or clarify their news releases, drawings or commentaries.

4. The Mediator Team determines the point in time when questioning and discussion should end and a resolution should be discussed. The Mediator Team then meets and discusses possible problem-solving ideas, while the rest of the class completes research using topics you have provided and works on the extension activities.

5. The Mediator Team then informs the group that a resolution has been made. The resolution is presented by the Lead Mediator.

6. The Who's Who teams listen to the resolution and then prepares a statement of approval or disapproval on the Closing Statement sheet (page 16).

7. The Lead Mediator then asks for each team's response, allowing for discussion.

8. After all responses have been heard, the Lead Mediator or the instructor reads *What Really Happened* to the entire class.

9. Who's Who teams then complete their Closing Statement sheet by recording their reaction to What Really Happened to their character in real life.

10. Evaluation and discussion about what has evolved during the hearing continues through the use of the *Yesterday Meets Today* activity sheet (page 17). All students may receive their own copy to complete or you or the Lead Mediator may use an overhead and complete the evaluation as a group.

Reminder: This is not to be a trial. This is to be a public hearing where all the people involved are given the chance to be respected and heard.

Summary of Roles and Worksheets

Role	number of students	Background Information	Meet the People Profiles	Diary Entries	Investigator Questions	Job Description- Mediator Team	Job Description - Who's Who	Job Description - Public Voice	Recorder Sheet	Who's Who and Why?	Interview Sheet	Letter to the Editor	Newspaper Layout	Closing Statement	Yesterday Meets Today	Extension Activities
Mediator Team																
Lead Mediator	1	*	*	*		*									*	
Recorder	1	*	*	*		*			*						*	
Investigators	3	*	*	*	*	*									*	
Who's Who Teams																
Character 1	3-5	*	*	*			*			*				*	*	*
Character 2	3-5	*	*	*			*			*				*	*	*
Character 3	3-5	*	*	*			*			*				*	*	*
Character 4	3-5	*	*	*			*			*				*	*	*
Public Voice																
Reporters	?	*	*					*			*		*		*	*
Photographers	?	*	*					*					*		*	*
Bystanders	?	*	*					*				*			*	*

Special Notes

The number of people performing the duties of the public voice depends on the number of students left over after other roles have been assigned.

The Mediator Team receives copies of all the diary entries. Each Who's Who Team receives only the diary for the character they are portraying.

The What Really Happened sheet can be read by the Lead Mediator or by the instructor.

Job Description
Mediator Team

The goal of the Mediator Team is to allow all persons being represented the opportunity to share their sides of the story. It is your job to encourage each side to be heard, showing your support and willingness to listen and not taking sides without listening to everyone first. You have to listen to each side openly and respectfully. After you have heard each side's position, your team will try to find a nonviolent solution that will be fair to as many people as possible.

While working as a team to bring out the different points of view and finding a resolution that is fair to as many people as possible, you will be assigned one of these jobs.

Lead Mediator - Your job is to monitor the hearing.

1. You allow the Investigators to ask the Who's Who characters their questions and approve or disapprove further questions the Investigators may have prepared.

2. You bring the audience back to the focus of the discussion if they seem to get off the track.

3. Allow all sides an equal amount of time and a fair opportunity to share their points of view.

4. After hearing all sides of the conflict, lead your team through a problem-solving discussion to reach a resolution for the crisis at hand.

5. Read the resolution to the audience.

6. Listen to each Who's Who team's comments on the resolution.

7. Read *What Really Happened* to the audience.

8. Ask for comments. Complete the *Yesterday Meets Today* activity sheet together, encouraging discussion.

Recorder - Your job is to keep an ongoing record of the hearing. Your duties will be to record facts and feelings that will be helpful to the Mediator Team. Record information about each character and his or her point of view, responses to questions, and events that affect the character.

Investigators - Your job involves bringing out the various points of view of each character by asking questions.

1. Enter the hearing with an open mind. Do not make any pre-judged decisions until all the stories have been heard. Listen to the presentations by each character.

2. Read over the material you are given and prepare questions for the Who's Who members. Remember to look at the story from all sides.

3. Ask each team their questions, alternating between characters to avoid being repetitious.

Job Description
Who's Who

For every story in the history books, there are at least two sides. History is full of dates, facts and events that have been recorded in our books. What often seems to get left in the past, though, are the many differing emotions involved in these historical events.

This is your chance to become a part of history and see an event from a different point of view, from another side of the story. Your job involves bringing one point of view to life. You will work in a small group to represent one character and the character's viewpoint.

1. Choose a spokesman for your group.

2. Take on the thoughts and feelings of your Who's Who character wholeheartedly, even though it may mean putting your beliefs aside for awhile.

3. Read over the *Background Information*, the *Meet the People* material, your *Investigator Questions*, and your *Diary Entry* until you can confidently represent your historical figure at the hearing.

4. Use the *Who's Who and Why?* sheet to make note of key statements or important comments you want to remember to use when you are being questioned at the hearing. You want the people around you to hear your ideas over and over again, so they can truly understand why you feel the way you do. Present facts to illustrate or back up your beliefs so your story will be believable.

5. After the Mediator Team has decided on a way to solve the problem, listen to the resolution. Tell if you agree or disagree with this solution by recording your opinion on the *Closing Statement* sheet.

6. Listen to what actually happened with this historic dilemma. Record your reactions using the prompts at the bottom of the the *Closing Statement* sheet.

7. Offer your final input on the *Yesterday Meets Today* activity sheet.

Job Description
Public Voice

Throughout history, events have been recorded and, thus, have been passed on to later generations. There have always been some kind of news reporters who sought to "tell it like it was" so the public could be kept informed about events that affected them. Often there were also photographers and illustrators who captured specific moments of time in pictures to help us remember what happened. And then there were the bystanders, the heart of the public, who felt compelled to become a part of history's events by sharing their own ideas and thoughts through newspaper, radio or TV commentary. All these people have helped record history and preserve it for future generations.

News Reporters will be responsible for:

1. Interviewing Who's Who members to get acquainted with the various opinions being represented.

2. Summarizing the day's activities for a newspaper, radio or television broadcast. Be creative. You may work with other reporters or by yourself.

Photographers will be responsible for:

1. Taking actual photos or videos during the hearing, drawing scenes of the characters at the hearing, or creating cartoons to symbolize events or viewpoints.

2. Preparing all the visual representations to be used in the newspaper, radio or TV broadcasts.

Bystanders are responsible for:

1. Keeping an ongoing record of comments from Who's Who characters, the Mediator Team members, or your own ideas about the proceedings. These will be used to write a letter to the editor. Use the *Letter to the Editor Pre-Composing Notes* for this purpose.

2. Compose a letter to the editor, sharing your feelings about the crisis situation.

Recorder Sheet

Mediator Team Recorder _____

Crisis Hearing _____ Date _____

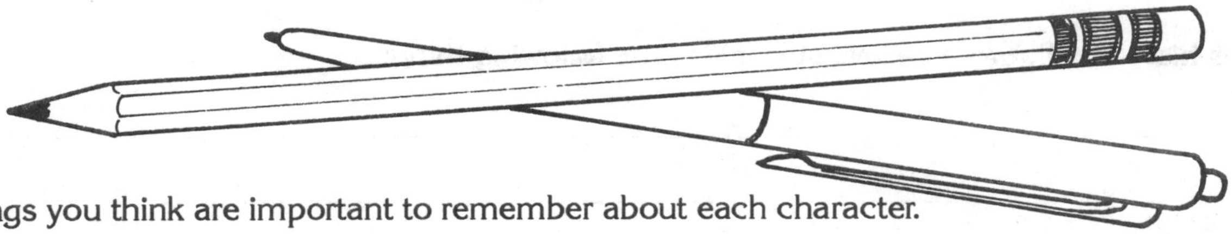

Record things you think are important to remember about each character.

Character 1 _____

_____

_____

_____

_____

Character 2 _____

_____

_____

_____

_____

Character 3 _____

_____

_____

_____

_____

Character 4 _____

_____

_____

_____

_____

Who's Who and Why?

In this Crisis Hearing _____ in the year _____

I am representing _____

As this historical figure, I believe strongly in the following things.

_____

_____

_____

_____

_____

_____

_____

_____

_____

_____

I base my beliefs on these facts and events.

1. _____

2. _____

3. _____

4. _____

5. _____

6. _____

7. _____

8. _____

9. _____

10. _____

Interview Sheet

News Reporter _____

Crisis Hearing_____ Date _____

Character interviewed _____

? ! ? ? / ! ! ? ? ! ? ! ? ?

Questions and Comments

1. What made you want to get involved in this conflict in the first place? _____

_____

_____

2. What do you see your role as being in this situation? _____

_____

_____

3. When do you feel the trouble first began? Why? _____

_____

_____

4. Who do you feel is most to blame in this crisis situation? Why?_____

_____

_____

_____

5. Who do you believe could save this situation from developing into something harmful? Why?

_____

_____

_____

LETTER TO THE EDITOR
Pre-Composing Notes

I am a bystander at the _____ Crisis Hearing.   The year is _____

My fictitious name is _____

These are the ideas I had about each character while listening to each side of the story.

Character 1 _____

_____

_____

_____

Character 2 _____

_____

_____

_____

Character 3 _____

_____

_____

_____

Character 4 _____

_____

_____

_____

Use these comments and ideas to
write a letter to the editor.

Daily Times

Vol. 1 - No. 1

⤹ headline

⤹ picture

⤹ story

Closing Statement

Crisis Hearing _____ Date _____

Character being represented _____

I have listened to the final resolution proposed by the Mediator Team.

☐ I approve of this resolution.

☐ I disapprove of this resolution.

These are my reasons:

_____
_____
_____
_____
_____
_____
_____
_____
_____
_____
_____

After you have listened to *What Really Happened*, which explains what happened to your character during this historic event, do one of the following:

- write out your thoughts randomly as they come to you
- make a list of adjectives that describe how you feel
- draw a picture to show how you feel
- develop a poem or song expressing your feelings
- create a statement that could one day become a famous quote

Yesterday Meets Today

Crisis Hearing_____ Date _____

Conflict _____

Who's Who Figures

Names   Beliefs

_____   _____

_____   _____

_____   _____

_____   _____

What really happened? _____

_____

_____

What should have happened? _____

_____

Why didn't it happen? _____

_____

_____

What could have been done to stop the confrontation from taking place? _____

_____

_____

_____

Discuss how the things you have learned in this unit could be used to avoid confrontations in your life.

Extension Activities

1. Character Research

Choose one of the people who were involved in this situation. Find as much information as you can about this person. Present your information in one of the following forms:

- a written report that includes at least one illustration
- a diary entry that the person might have written
- a monologue where you pretend to be the person and present his or her feelings on the topic you are studying
- a time line that shows the important events in his or her life.

2. Character Comparison

Choose two characters from this situation. Make a Venn diagram that compares the two people, listing characteristics of one person in one of the areas, the other person's personal attributes in the other area, and common characteristics in the overlapping area.

3. Personal Poster

Choose one of the characters from this situation. Make a poster about this person that depicts his or her achievements and topics on which he or she took a stand.

4. Setting

Research the area where this situation took place. Make a bulletin board, a mural, or a map that shows what the area was like. Mark all important landmarks, buildings or geographical features.

5. Illustrated Time Line

Make a time line that shows the sequence of events that contributed to this situation. Add symbols or illustrations for some of the events. If necessary, do additional research to document when each event happened and to add additional events that might not have been mentioned in the background information for this unit.

Extension Activities

6. Original Story

Write an original story that is set in the same time and location as the conflict you are studying. Your story may be fictional but should reflect some real events and/or people.

7. Letters to a Friend

Be one of the characters in this situation and write several letters to a friend explaining the events that you are experiencing and your feelings about the situation.

8. Diamante poem

Choose two opposing concepts from this unit (for instance, slavery and freedom, war and peace, or cooperation and defiance). Write a diamante poem with one of the concepts as the beginning word and the opposite concept as the last ending word. The poem should follow this form:

line 1 - *the subject (concept word 1)*
line 2 - *2 adjectives describing the subject*
line 3 - *3 ing-words describing the subject*
line 4 - *2 adjectives describing the first subject, a hyphen, and 2 adjectives about the opposing subject*
line 5 - *3 ing-words about the opposing subject*
line 6 - *2 adjectives describing the opposing subject*
line 7 - *the opposing subject (concept word 2)*

9. Commemorative Stamp

Design a stamp to commemorate this event or situation or to honor important people involved in this event. Write a paragraph describing why you feel this event or person deserves this honor.

10. Dramatic Reading

Deliver a dramatic reading of a speech or written commentary that one of the characters in this conflict originally presented. Explain the setting or context in which this person made this presentation.

Extension Activities

11. Display

Make a display that shows one or more of the following:

- an illustrated map
- illustrations of important characters
- an important building or location
- sample writings from one or more characters
- replicas of artifacts
- illustrations (with captions) of the most important events.

12. Monument

Design a monument to commemorate the event or an important person involved in the conflict. Explain the significance of the monument.

13. Written or Oral Report

Make a list of places, people, and things related to this historic event. Choose one and do additional research. Present your findings in a written or oral report. Include illustrations or visual aids to make your report more interesting.

14. Collage

Choose one person, place or concept related to this historic event. Make a collage of pictures and sayings that communicates the important ideas about this person or thing.

15. Scrapbook

Choose one of the important characters. Create a scrapbook that this person might have made to record his or her thoughts and preserve important mementos of the event.

THE PEQUOT WAR
Background Information

The first people arrived in America thousands of years ago; some authorities feel as early as 20,000 to 40,000 B.C. Centuries of life took place in America long before any white settlers arrived to "discover" it.

The Algonquins

The Native Americans settled in various places. The Algonquin tribes settled in the woodlands along the east coast of what we know now as the New England states. These Indians lived in forests where every tree became a brother or friend. The forest supplied all of their needs — food, clothing, shelter, and medicine. The Algonquin never took the life of a tree or forest animal without reason; a use was found for everything.

There were several Algonquian-speaking tribes that lived in the New England woodlands from Maine to Virginia. Even though they were in different tribes, they all came from the same background. Because of this mutual heritage, their language, political ways, religious beliefs, economics, social structure and customs were basically the same.

The Pequot Indians, an Algonquin tribe from the Hudson River area, emigrated to the Connecticut Valley in the early 1600s to escape the vicious Iroquois, the severe weather, and land limitations. The smaller Algonquin tribes in the valley, the Narragansetts, Mohegans and Niantics, did not like the Pequot's forceful ways. Pequot means "destroyer." The Pequot people felt that this meant they were leaders, stronger and wiser than the other tribes. The other tribes did not feel this way. The Pequots soon became their enemy.

The Wampanoag tribe lived northeast of the other tribes. The Wampanoag chief at that time was Massasoit, meaning "great one." He had heard stories of the white settlers kidnapping young warriors from a nearby village, Patuxet, and taking them to a place called England. He was thankful his tribe was not closer to the coast.

The Great Sickness

Massasoit had good relations with other tribes. They came to him often for advice and support. One day, a messenger from the Massachusetts tribe came to see Massasoit at Sowams. He brought with him two tattered white men as a gift, to be given to the great sachem.

The messenger told Massasoit that his people had traded with these white men. "They wanted our beaver skins," he said, "but they cheated my people and even killed one of us. We went to the ship at night, killed the white men and took six captives. We give these two to you, Massasoit."

Massasoit accepted the captives and put them to work. After a short time, one man fell gravely ill. He had smallpox and he infected the entire tribe with the deadly disease. The Great Sickness had begun.

Before the Great Sickness, there were some 100,000 Algonquins living in the woodlands. By 1617, over 95,000 had died; so many that there were not enough strong tribal members to bury those who had died. Once flourishing communities in the rich, forest-filled lands were now silent and empty.

English Settlers

The White people continued to come to the New World. Spain had been the world power for years, and now that the Dutch and British had finally defeated the Spanish, the rest of Europe was eager to be a part of this New World expedition. It offered so much – future trade, opportunity, and expansion of power.

Troubled by King James and his ideals, many English people wished for freedom of religion; a chance to practice their beliefs without persecution. They believed that they needed to be separated from the Church of England instead of trying to change it.

Earlier, in 1609 a group of these *Separatists* had left England to live in the more accepting Holland. There they lived comfortably for 11 years. Eventually even in Holland they began to feel religious tension.

In August of 1620 the Separatists, or *Pilgrims*, left Holland bound for the New World. The Pilgrims traveled in search of religious freedom, while others were in search of adventure. Traveling on the *Mayflower*, William Bradford and others wrote the Mayflower Compact. All 41 adults signed it, agreeing that the Pilgrims would govern their future community.

Arriving in a spacious and protected harbor during winter, the Pilgrims decided to stay on board their ship for a while rather than battle the winter in an unknown land. Sending out scouts, the adventurers found baskets filled with corn hidden on the beach. They were extremely thankful for the food.

On board the *Mayflower*, scurvy and other illnesses made the Pilgrims' first winter a devastating one. Over half their company died, leaving a mere 50 people by the end of the winter to begin their new community. By February, there were only seven able-bodied survivors to carry the others onto land. They chose land already cleared and protected from all sides. They called it Plymouth.

Massasoit and the Pilgrims

A young Patuxet warrior, kidnapped a few years earlier and taken to England, had been returned to his village only to find that his tribe had been killed off by the Great Sickness. His name was Squanto. He left the empty village of Patuxet and went to live with Massasoit at Sowams.

Squanto had been living with Massasoit and his people in Sowams for about 6 months. Massasoit knew the white people had set up camp at Plymouth. He often sent guides to keep track of the new settlers.

March 16, 1620, Massasoit sent his guide Samoset to meet the Pilgrims, because Samoset knew some English. The Pilgrims learned a lot from Samoset. They gave him gifts and asked to meet with his sachem (leader), Massasoit. Massasoit agreed to meet with the Pilgrims. Squanto went with them.

The Wampanoag sachem and the Pilgrim leader made peace with each other. They established a treaty and smoked a peace pipe to honor their treaty.

Massasoit returned to Sowams, some 40 miles away. Squanto stayed with the Pilgrims. He taught them how to grow corn, where and how to fish and hunt, and much more. He was invaluable to this young community.

By fall, the Pilgrims had produced a harvest of corn. In a celebration for a plentiful harvest, the Pilgrims and Indians shared the first Thanksgiving together in the fall of 1621.

The Puritans

The land in the New World was available for development. Dutch and European ships arrived with settlers anxious for a new beginning and with traders eager to profit from fur trading.

Eight years later in England, another religious group was eager to leave the restraints of the throne and England's anti-Puritan ways. The *Puritans* did not want to separate from the Church of England. They wanted to change it by being an example to others of pure Christianity. They felt they were God's chosen people, given a unique opportunity to seek out new lands and direct the young nation to follow their way of life.

Arriving in Massachusetts Bay, John Winthrop was elected the first Puritan governor. They named their new home Boston. Bringing tools the Pilgrims had lacked, their community prospered. They became skilled fisherman. Governor Winthrop kept in close contact with Governor Bradford, the governor of Plymouth. He often traveled two days along the coastal path to discuss with Bradford settlement growth, news from England, and relationships with the Natives.

Increases in population meant the white settlements needed to expand. The settlers' views on owning and settling land differed greatly from the Indians' views. Official deeds were made to show land purchased from the Indians through trade, but the settlers' understanding of these trades was sometimes different from the Native Americans' understanding.

Tensions Mount

In 1633, the Dutch purchased the Connecticut Valley land from the Pequots. Land near this great river would prove invaluable for inland trade. To these adventurers, this land seemed to never end. Forests, tremendous soil, endless water — truly the Land of Opportunity!

The trade forced the Pequots to move south, sending them deeper into their neighbor's hunting grounds. Trading continued, but the Indians were becoming more cautious and demanding as they learned the true worth of the white man's gifts. Their land was being traded for trinkets.

Some traders were hostile and took Indians captive for the slave trade. Tensions mounted. Two traders, Captain Stone and Captain Oldham, had been killed by the Pequots for their unfair trading practices. In turn, the Massachusetts Bay Colony sent soldiers to scare off these Indians, the only real threat to colonial expansion.

The Pequots went to their neighbors trying to convince them of the unfair ways of the whites. "They are not to be trusted!" they shouted. "We need to make peace with each other and send the white man back. Let us make peace!"

The smaller Algonquin tribes, howver, depended on trading with the white people. So far they had not broken their peace treaty with the white settlers. The Pequot would remain the enemy of these smaller tribes. These tribes would side with the settlers rather than joining the Pequot.

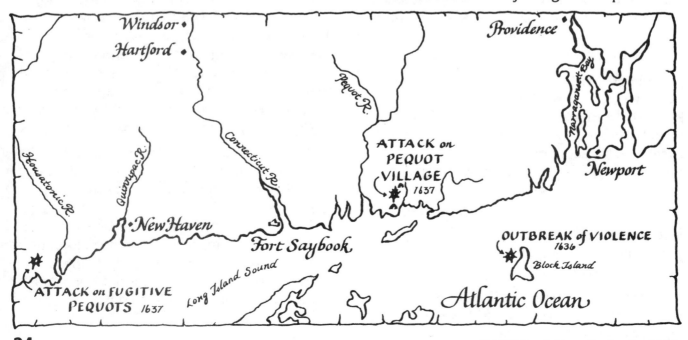

William Bradford

William Bradford, governor of the Plymouth Company for 30 years, began his life in Austerfield, Yorkshire, in England, in March, 1590. Even as a young boy, Bradford was interested in politics, which at that time meant being active in the church. At the age of 12, during the peak of the Protestant Reformation, Bradford joined the Separatist Church, the "left wing" and more vocal side of Puritanism.

At 19 Bradford joined others seeking refuge from the Church of England and traveled to Holland in search of a happier life. There they found people who let them live their lives as they chose. They lived there for 11 years.

The people in Bradford's group wanted to stay together, but finding work in Holland was difficult. Young and hopeful, Bradford organized a trip to the New World in 1620. On the trip across the Atlantic, 30-year-old Bradford and the others planned out their new government by writing the Mayflower Compact.

The next year Bradford was unanimously chosen to govern the settlement called Plymouth. He was reelected 30 times, serving almost every year between 1621 and 1656.

Bradford had taught himself to read and write as a child and never missed the opportunity to learn more. He listened to people speak other languages, read all available books, and wrote an account of the Pilgrim's travels. He was hardworking and strong-willed, yet remained honest and open with his fellow Pilgrims and the Wampanoag people. He showed a lot of compassion and sensitivity to the struggles each person had to endure. In the challenging New World Bradford was always one of the first to pitch in and do his share of the work.

John Winthrop

John Winthrop was born on January 12, 1588 in Suffolk, England. The Winthrop family had strong beliefs as Puritans. They led a pure and honest life. They differed from the Separatists, though, because they did not want to break away from the Church of England even though they were persecuted by members of the Church of England. They believed that they were God's chosen people, His persecuted and beloved followers, who would act as examples for others to follow.

To find a more peaceful life and continue to change the lives of others, John Winthrop and other Puritans set sail for the New World in 1629 on the *Arabella*. While traveling across the Atlantic, Winthrop used the time to write out his reasons for leaving England and also write a plan for the colony they would build in the New World. Entitled, *A Model of Christian Charity*, Winthrop based his beliefs on Bible passages, claiming the group's divine right to occupy and control land in the New World.

Winthrop was 42 years old when he and others reached the New World at Massachusetts Bay. They named their settlement Boston. Winthrop was first elected governor in 1630 and was elected 12 other times during the next 19 years until his death in 1649 at age 61.

As governor, Winthrop led his people with determination and strength, basing his beliefs and commitment on God's word. He reminded them daily that they were a special people, responsible for others who did not live as pure lives as they did. It was the Puritans' duty to lead and direct all those in need of guidance. He did not encourage relations with the Algonquin unless it involved trading for land.

Sassacus

Sassacus had been on the move most of his life. Born in the late 1500s near the Hudson River, his Algonquin people, the Pequots, had been persecuted by the fierce Iroquois tribes in that area. Seeking a better life, Sassacus's father led his people east to the Connecticut Valley. Used to defending themselves, the Pequots continued to be aggressive towards others, expecting their new neighbors, smaller Algonquin tribes in the area, to choose them as the lead tribe.

Sassacus became tribal leader in the new settlement in the Connecticut Valley. He found resources for hunting, fishing and farming. A tall, muscular man, Sassacus was born of leaders to become a leader. He would not desert his people. He would provide for his people, the proud Algonquins, Dwellers Among the Leaves.

Sassacus watched as white men settled in their area. They originally settled in Plymouth, but in time they slowly moved inland. Eventually trading was established between the white men and the Pequots.

On June 8, 1633 the white settlers bought some land from Sassacus in the Connecticut Valley. They paid for the land with tools and special gifts. Sassacus told his people that they had to move to the Mystic River. They would find good fishing and hunting there, for it was still land of the great Algonquin tribe. The Mohegans and Narragansetts were also living in that area, but the land was vast. The other tribes, he assured them, would be pleased that his Pequot people would be there to protect and guide them. The other tribes, however, did not feel this way. Sassacus was confused.

At first Sassacus found trading with the whites helpful. The tools the Pequots received enabled them to hunt, fish, and live a better life. Then the Pequots began to doubt the white people. The white people tricked the Pequots and killed their warriors. Sassacus became worried. He could not let this continue. He felt that he had to bring other tribal leaders together to discuss the problem.

Massasoit

Massasoit was chief of the Wampanoags, an Algonquin tribe. It seemed that he had always been the chief. Living in the woodland of today's Rhode Island and Massachusetts areas, near the eastern and northern coasts of Narragansett Bay, the Wampanoags lived a peaceful life. Massasoit had only known the peacefulness and friendship that his people shared with nature and the neighboring tribes.

Life began to change for Massasoit as he saw the Pequots enter the area. The Pequots were a strong and active people. Massasoit did not encourage a relationship with the Pequots. Throughout his life he had learned that in time all storms would pass, and he figured that someday the Pequots, too, would move on. He encouraged the other tribes to do the same.

Then the white settlers came to the area in the 1620s. Since the settlers had few resources, Massasoit and his people helped them. The Wampanoag people welcomed the new people, gave them food, and helped them learn about the land.

Gentle yet just, Massasoit continued to foster his relationship with the new settlers. He found them to be appreciative and conscientious. He saw in them a hope for the future for all peoples living in their lands. Although devastated by the Great Sickness, he knew that the white men had not intended on killing so many people with this sickness. Massasoit opened trade relations with the settlers. They offered tools, gifts, and services for the items they needed. Although life had been changed by their presence, living alongside the white people was not too bad.

THE PEQUOT WAR

Investigator Questions

The following are questions you may use in questioning the Who's Who team members. Add some questions of your own, being careful to be fair and to allow each side of the story to be shared.

Questions for Massasoit, the Wampanoag leader

1. When the Pilgrims first arrived, you sent scouts out to watch them. Why did you want to meet them?

2. Why did you leave Squanto with the Pilgrims that first year?

3. What are your reasons for not encouraging your people and other Algonquin tribes to accept the Pequots?

4. You have traded with the Pilgrims for over 15 years. You have not broken your treaty, but you have heard what has happened between the white settlers and other Algonquin tribes. How does it make you feel to hear stories about the whites taking advantage, even killing, your Algonquin people?

Add your own questions.

_____

_____

_____

Questions for Sassacus, the Pequot leader

1. Your people have been searching for a home for many years now. Why did you move to the Mystic River where other Algonquin tribes lived?

2. How are your people different from the Wampanoags, Narragansetts, Niantics, and the Mohegans?

3. Some tribes continue to trade with the white settlers. How do you feel about this?

4. What would you like to see happen to the white people living in the Connecticut Valley?

Add your own questions

_____

_____

_____

Pequot War Questions, continued

Questions for William Bradford, the Plymouth governor

1. You left your family and friends in England and then again in Holland. Why did you come to the New World?

2. Why do you think the treaty between you and Massasoit has lasted so long?

3. You have always been a good writer and communicator. In your many letters to friends back in England, you must have written about Massasoit and his Wampanoag people. How did you describe them? What did you say about them?

4. You see the Pequots as a threat to the Algonquin and white settlers in the area. Why?

Add your own questions.

_____

_____

_____

_____

Questions for John Winthrop, governor of Boston

1. Why did you leave England?

2. When you stepped off the *Arabella* in 1630 at Massachusetts Bay to find a land already cleared and open, you knew this would be the land you would settle on. Why?

3. The natives you have come in contact with do not like you. They say you do not look them in the eye and you have not tried to learn their language and communicate with them. Why do you act this way toward them?

4. After Captain Oldham was killed, soldiers were sent from Massachusetts Bay Colony to destroy Pequot land and cattle. How did this make you feel?

Add your own questions.

_____

_____

_____

_____

William Bradford

May 1637

I have been governor of Plymouth since its beginning 15 years ago. I have seen an eager group of people leave England and then Holland, in search of religious freedom. Out of over 100 passengers on the Mayflower, only 50 of us survived. Life was extremely difficult for a long time. Squanto, a special instrument sent by God, taught us how to set corn, where to fish, and how to make needed items out of what was around us. Times were hard.

I have encouraged our many settlers to seek out new places to build their communities. The coastal areas offer abundant trading, as do the river areas leading inland.

Massasoit and his Wampanoag people have been good to us. Our peace treaty has remained strong. He seems open to giving the settlers more land to explore and in which to expand. He feels his people do not own the land; they only hunt and fish on it.

I have heard of Indian troubles inland. We have built a fort as a precaution. I have heard that the Pequots feel hostile toward the English at Connecticut. Two traders, Captain Stone and Captain Oldham, have been killed by the Pequots. The English called their friends and confederates in the Bay of Massachusetts to send them speedy aid. Captain Endicott and his men gave a quick and strong show of force to the Pequots, destroying crops and cattle.

The Pequots are known to be forceful. They are large in number and are the only true threat to the settlers here. The Wampanoags, Narragansetts and other tribes seem willing to continue the trading with us. Tensions are brewing though. Something will need to be done about the violent Pequots.

Massasoit

May 1637

I sent Mr. Winslow, a messenger from Plymouth, back to his home at Plymouth at high noon. He comes often to see me. His people and I made a peace treaty when the Pilgrims first came here. We have continued to honor the treaty. I became ill once and almost died. Mr. Winslow brought me white man's medicine and I lived. Our fur trading and peace has lasted for many years.

I have lived 40 years now. My wife and I have made a good home for our two sons and one daughter. The Wampanoag people live happy lives. We hunt well. Our forest gives us everything we need. The white traders like the furs we give them. My people smile when they see the traders' kettles, jewelry and tools. The women are happy to wear dresses of red. The white people have a lot of things we can use.

Many tribes do not like the white people, but I tell them all is well. The Pilgrims are good.

My eyes and ears do not see everything. My son, who Governor Bradford gave the name Philip, talks of great troubles ahead. He sees too many whites and not many Indians. I have given a lot of land to the white settlers living in the area. They settle on these lands as the white man do. We live and hunt in the forest around them as we learned to do. We have taught the white people many things about living in this land. I feel sure that they will keep the peace that we made when our eyes first met.

My son talks of trouble with Pequots on the Mystic River. Narragansett, Niantic, and Mohegan sachems will meet with me soon to talk about this problem.

Diary Entry

Sassacus

May 1637

I am a Pequot. We are destroyers. It is our way of life. We are good hunters. We are strong and determined. We do not bow down to anyone. We are leaders and should lead all Algonquin tribes. The Great Chieftain is proud of us.

The white people are evil. They come to take from our land, our trees, our waters, and our people. They only want; they do not give. Their trade is not true. Their gifts are small. The gifts do not match the beauty and power of what they take from us. I do not trust the white man. If we burn their houses and kill their cattle, they will go back to their first land.

I want to make peace with my Indian Brothers. Once enemies, we now need to choose only between Indian and white. We live and share the woods here while the whites take over our river lands. Our hunting grounds are small now. We must find peace to live together and push the white settlers back. They will take everything from us until there is nothing left to take.

I try to tell the other tribal leaders this. I see their eyes lower to the ground. Their hearts are heavy. I know they feel my words are true, yet they are a proud people. They see us still as outsiders, a people who came into their land uninvited so many years ago. We were great in number and needed to hunt and feed more people than they. We became enemies only because we needed to survive.

Are the white people not outsiders too?

What will happen to my people? To my wife, son and daughter? I cannot take them anywhere. We have no place to go.

Diary Entry

John Winthrop

May 1637

As I look out my door, I feel truly blessed. Boston, now in its 7th year, has proven itself pleasing to the Lord. I feel that the placing of our people in this country came directly from God. We are God's chosen people. With our pure thoughts and pure ways, we will continue to be a model of Christian charity. This young nation will learn from us.

When coming to this land, we found beautifully prepared lands welcoming us. The Great Sickness had eliminated the savages who had lived in these lands. We were destined to arrive here and begin our Puritan world.

Acting as governor here, I have striven to guide the Puritans of Massachusetts Bay justly. We are to walk in God's light and keep His commandments so that He will bless us in the land we choose to settle. We strive for perfection.

The Indians we come in contact with are savages. We do not feel these beings should own land. They do not understand the meaning of the word. They live in strange homes, grow tribal crop areas, and work as one. How can they expect to improve themselves? How can they expect to survive? They have no money, no education, and no belief in the one true God. They are heathens!

Such savages are the Pequots on Block Island who killed Captain Oldham on his trading ship a few weeks ago. The settlers there begged for our military action. I sent Captain Endicott and his men to the island. They burned the Pequot's crops. We will not allow any future problems from these savages.

The Pequots seem the greatest threat to the settlers here. They are destroyers. God will allow us to deal with them as we choose.

THE PEQUOT WAR

What Really Happened

Captain Stone was killed by Pequots in 1634. Captain Oldham was killed in the spring of 1636. Both had been known for their cheating ways and illegal trading with the English and Dutch in New England. They were dishonest and self-serving; eager only to make a profit.

Captain Oldham's ship had anchored at Block Island, home to some Pequot Indians, across from Narragansett Bay where more Pequots, Narragansetts, Mohegans and Niantics lived.

It was night time during the spring of 1636. Another trading ship was also passing Block Island and saw and heard Oldham's ship being ransacked by Indians. The other English ship rammed Oldham's vessel, sending several Indians into the water to drown. Shots were fired at the intruders as they tried to flee. As the rescuing English boarded the ship, they found several dead, including Captain Oldham. Had he been killed by the Pequots in revenge for his cruel trading, or had he been shot by one of his own countrymen from the rescue ship?

The soldiers at Massachusetts Bay Colony came as soon as they could, sometime during the early summer months after being requested by the Connecticut settlers living close to Block Island and Narragansett Bay. Their boats traveled directly to Block Island where they burned the Pequot cornfields and killed their cattle. The Pequots were not killed because they had hidden themselves in the trees and swamps.

The soldiers had come and gone quickly, leaving a devastated land behind. The settlers at Narragansett Bay had been thankful for the soldiers' actions, but felt very much alone after they had returned home to tend their own crops. What would they do with the angry Pequots now?

The Pequots searched out peace with the neighboring tribes. Sassacus met with the other tribal leaders and presented his position passionately.

"They are strangers in our country," Sassacus told the other tribal leaders. "They are everywhere and will overthrow you all in time."

The Narragansetts were willing to listen. Not all their encounters with the white men had been good. Their life had changed a lot. Maybe Sassacus spoke the truth.

The Narragansett sachem could not forget the experiences with the Pequot tribe, however. They had wronged his people and the other tribes in the area. Trade was strong with the white man. The Pequot were the enemy, not the white man. They finally decided they would join the white settlers in their fight against the Pequots.

The Pequots, angered and frustrated, began to taunt the settlers. They killed their cattle and burned their storage sheds, creating further tensions. The Pequot felt that if the white men had no food in the winter, they could be forced back to their homes across the seas. The plan was sure to work.

As the winter turned to spring, spirits rose within the English communities. They vowed revenge on the Pequots.

During May of 1637, Captain John Mason of Connecticut, began planning an attack on this most feverish Indian tribe. The Pequots were the only true threat to their New

England colonies. The attack would take place on May 25.

Around 4 o'clock in the morning Captain Mason, about 90 English settlers, and over 300 Indian allies departed for the Pequot's main village at Mystic River. They were organized and were "eager to see their longtime enemy humbled."

The Indian allies led them to the sleeping village. They surrounded the camp, allowing Captain Mason and his troops to make the actual attack. Most Pequots had no chance to escape. Some who tried to escape were massacred by the waiting Indians. The troops set fire to everything. In a very short time, over 600 Pequot men, women and children had been murdered.

The Narragansett sachem had requested the head of Sassacus as proof of the final destruction of the tribe. Sassacus and 200 others had escaped. Where had they gone?

Deep in the forest, Sassacus, his family, and others tried desperately to survive. Revengeful, they captured and killed the family of the Mohegan sachem, Uncus.

Sassacus then led his followers to the shores of Narragansett Bay. They tried to hide in the swamps, but the English found them. In the foggy swamp, 180 surrendered and then watched as their mighty Sassacus and his warriors were killed. Beheaded by Indians, his scalp was given to the English as a commitment to friendship.

The Pequots who surrendered were sold into the Bermuda slave trade or given to the Narragansett, Mohegan or Niantic tribes as a prize for helping them avenge the Pequots. The mighty Pequot nation had been destroyed.

Sassacus' words rang true, however. In 1671, 34 years later, led by Massasoit's son, Philip, the Indians united to fight the white colonists. Over 50,000 colonists lived in New England at this time, while there were only 20,000 Indians. The Puritans won the fight easily.

The Boston Tea Party

Background Information

English Debt

Tensions between Great Britain and the colonies had been brewing for quite some time. The French and Indian War had ended peacefully in 1763, granting Great Britain greater control of lands in America, yet leaving the British with incredible wartime debts.

King George wondered where he would get the money to pay for all of the ammunition, ships, and other wartime costs. He had spent years transporting, feeding, clothing and maintaining British soldiers in hopes of gaining more land in the Americas. The British had quadrupled their land holdings in America and had completely ousted the French, but at a great cost. King George needed lots of income immediately.

American Taxes

After much deliberation, King George felt it would be both necessary and reasonable to tax the American colonists. What could the colonists say in response? After all, these colonists were of British descent. They were British citizens and, therefore, did not have a choice whether or not to obey these laws; they were expected to obey them as were all other citizens of the British Empire.

King George based his reasoning on the following laws:

1. The law stated, "All persons born in any part of the King's dominions and within his protection are his subjects, as all those born in Ireland, Scotland, Wales, the King's plantations, or on the English seas, . . . and truly, by birth they are British citizens, as their descendants are."

2. ". . . all the King's subjects, both in Great Britain and in the colonies and plantations in America, have the right to the same general and essential privileges of the British constitution." It was the colonies' right to protection and wartime strength that had given the King such debts.

3. " . . . in order that the King's subjects in the colonies and plantations in America might have and enjoy the same liberties . . . it is necessary that the colonies should be vested with the authority and power of legislation." King George had appointed his finest men to govern his subjects across the Atlantic. He felt the colonists were being represented as equally as could be expected given the distance between them.

Thus, he reasoned, taxing the colonists would be a fair choice in attempting to diminish the national debt.

Taxation Without Representation

The colonists despised being taxed by a government that lay across the Atlantic Ocean. Parliament, which was located three thousand miles from their American homes, met, discussed, and decided the future of their colonial lives. How dare they do this! This was "taxation without representation" they argued.

The colonists tried desperately to involve themselves in the decision-making. They pleaded with England to allow them to send representatives to Parliament. Written and personal messages were sent, hoping for acceptance. Whether it was major communication problems or simply trying to ignore the situation, King George did not respond to their pleas. The colonists wanted answers quickly, and having to wait for word as it traveled across the seas did not make the waiting, nor the reply once it was returned, any more acceptable. Conflict between the mother country and the colonies began to intensify. They were both looking after their own self-interests. Both sides had arguments that supported their feelings and actions.

Taxing the Colonists

The first tax, the **Stamp Act**, was first collected in November 1765. It taxed everything made of paper — newspapers, diplomas, marriage licenses, etc. Nothing was legal without the required stamp, and the colonists had to pay to get the stamps. Unfortunately for Parliament, the stamp tax affected the lawyers, publishers and tavern keepers the most; the people who were more educated and vocal than the rest of the general public. These people knew what to say and how to say it. Severe protests were sent

across the Atlantic and within five months the Stamp Act had been repealed.

King George still needed money, though, and levied a new tax, the **Townsend Revenue Act** that taxed paint, paper, glass and tea. The colonists were furious. How dare the British tax their precious tea! That was the last straw. The colonists vowed they would not purchase anything that came from Great Britain.

The British merchants soon began losing money. Trade throughout the colonies dropped to practically nothing.

King George, sympathetic to the loyal merchants, and also working with a newly established and more compromising Parliament, lifted all the taxes except the one on the tea, hoping to resolve the situation.

The Colonists Rebel

Samuel Adams would not let the colonists be fooled. They would not be tricked into accepting this new law if it meant still being taxed for tea. Paying any tax on any import was wrong.

Led by the Sons of Liberty, the colonists refused to pay the tax on the ships waiting in the harbor. One ship, the *Dartmouth*, captained by Francis Rotch, had been anchored in Boston Harbor the longest and was getting desperate to unload her cargo. Rotch protested that he knew nothing of this duel between the colonists and the King and that he only needed to collect his payment, deposit his tea and be on his way. He did not want to get involved in any of it. A Quaker, Rotch tried desperately to seek out a solution.

Governor Hutchinson, having fled Boston for the safety of his country home in Milton, was determined to wait out these rowdy patriots. They would lose their ambition soon. There were too few of them to go against Great Britain, the beloved mother country.

Samuel Adams

A soft-spoken man of 51 years, Samuel Adams had become known as the colonial master of political persuasion. He could say anything to anyone. He considered the individual rights and freedoms of his fellow colonists his single goal in life; nothing else mattered. Looking rather worn and tattered if you saw him, Adams didn't seem to care. Eyes of steel gray, a long full nose and thin lips shaped the face of a kind, listening friend.

A strict Puritan, Adams truly believed that everything he did, he did for the Lord. He had few needs, yet an incredible passion for the common good of God's people in America.

Adams' father had been a well-to-do malt dealer, but Samuel did not follow in his father's footsteps. He had no business sense, which meant that he never became wealthy. He was, rather, a full-time rebel who received no pay for what he did. Although a Harvard graduate, he had never been able to keep a job for very long. People often wondered how his wife, Betsy, managed to feed and clothe herself and the children.

A hero he was not. Yet, no one could question his commitment. He formed the Sons of Liberty (a semi-secret organization of activists), began the Committees for Correspondence (a network of communication between the larger cities and outlying towns), and regularly visited taverns and meeting houses wearing his red cloak, eager to listen and encourage patriotism.

He organized the people of Boston against Great Britain, actively sought out opportunities to attack the king, and became the leader the patriots needed to stand up to the English throne.

Thomas Hutchinson

A native-born American, Hutchinson had been appointed governor three years prior to the conflict over the tea tax. Born to one of Boston's oldest and wealthiest families, Hutchinson graduated from Harvard and entered the world of politics, like his father and grandfather. He was a tall, handsome fellow with hazel eyes and a fair complexion. He carried his title and responsibility well; he wasn't arrogant, yet he had great confidence in himself.

The governor had two sons, Thomas and Elisha, who both worked for the East India Tea Company. Thomas had married into the family of one of Boston's most loyal tea importers. Loyalty to the throne was not a question in this household.

Governor Hutchinson, proud man that he was, had heard rumors of increased unrest among the Sons of Liberty, but he felt strongly that a challenge against the royal government must never take place. He would not let that happen. Too many of his Tory friends and their livelihoods were threatened. He could not back down to these patriots. Call it loyalty or stubbornness, he would not disappoint his king or his friends in Boston. He would give his full support to the tea agents. After all, what did these simple patriots have in their favor? Castle William, the fortress island three miles from Boston, held British soldiers as well as two men-of-war ships, the *Active* and the *Kingfisher*, ready for battle. Governor Hutchinson felt confident that the ships and soldiers would handle any uprising the patriots might start. All would be well.

Quaker Francis Rotch

Born in 1734 in Nantucket, Rotch grew up in the constant calm of a Quaker home. True pacifists, the Quakers went about their lives peacefully, avoiding any political conflicts.

Rotch's family became involved in the shipping business and William quickly became one of the more prominent Quaker ship owners. He was a smart ship owner and merchant and soon became wealthy. He and his wife Elizabeth lived in Nantucket with their five children.

Rotch continued to avoid the activities of the colonists in their fight for independence. He did not feel any loyalty to either side. He was a simple man, a hard-working man who tried very hard to live in peace with those around him. He did not dress in bright colors or fancy silks. He dared not speak out of turn, but rather spoke respectfully so as not to make anyone feel ashamed for what they felt or said. He belonged to neither the Tories (British loyalists) nor to the Whigs (those wanting independence from the throne). He was a businessman trying desperately to make a living.

Rotch continued his schedule of shipping goods from Great Britain to the colonists as usual. He had heard rumors in London that the colonists were becoming more active in their desire for independence, but he paid no attention to the rumor. He felt that if only people would learn to get along and work together instead of battling each other over who had more rights, things would be fine. He decided to stay out of the problem and just do his job.

He set sail for Boston. His ship, the *Dartmouth*, would lead both the *Eleanor* and the *Beaver* back to Boston harbor. There they would unload their cargo of tea, claim their pay and head back to London. He had enough food on board to last the round-trip voyage. Then, possibly, he would be able to spend some time in Nantucket with Elizabeth and his children.

𝕭𝖔𝖘𝖙𝖔𝖓 𝕿𝖊𝖆 𝕻𝖆𝖗𝖙𝖞

Investigator Questions

The following are questions you may use in questioning the Who's Who team members. Add some questions of your own, being careful to be fair and to allow each side of the story to be shared.

Questions for Samuel Adams, American patriot

1. Why do you feel the colonists deserve their independence?

2. Why do you continue to be a patriot leader even though it pays nothing?

3. What have the colonists done to show the King they are capable of governing and prospering by themselves?

4. What is your main motivation for doing what you do?

Add your own questions.

_____

_____

_____

_____

Questions for Governor Hutchinson, governor of Massachusetts

1. Why do you feel the colonists should remain loyal to their mother country, Great Britain?

2. Your father, grandfather, and great-grandfather all played a part in colonial politics, each remaining true to their king. What advice do you think they would give you now as you face a threatened throne?

3. Besides the king, who else do you represent or work for? How do you balance your obligations to the English throne and to the colonists?

4. What are your plans if military action is necessary?

Add your own questions.

_____

_____

_____

_____

Boston Tea Party Questions, continued

Questions for Quaker Francis Rotch, ship captain

1. What do you do for a living?
2. You seem to be caught in the middle of all this. What would you like Mr. Adams and his Whig friends and Governor Hutchinson and his Tory friends to know about your predicament?
3. You are a simple man who works hard at what he does. What do you expect from the colonists in America? from the British government?
4. What was your plan when you left London with a cargo of tea and headed for Boston?

Add your own questions.

____

____

____

____

Diary Entry

Samuel Adams

Thursday, December 16, 1773

Here it is, 6:30 in the evening. The rain has stopped. The skies are clearing. I am comforted by my oversized Newfoundland, Queue, on this most controversial night.

I feel strongly that most colonists are in support of any legal and reasonable protest against this tea tax. After tonight's meeting at Old South Hall, I know they will back me if more drastic measures need to be taken. Through the Committees of Correspondence, we were able to recruit people from nearly 21 miles away to attend our meeting.

I felt badly about having to send Quaker Rotch out in the pouring rain to go talk with Governor Hutchinson, but what other choice did we have? Everyone knew today was the deadline. Something had to be done today, and even though we had tried to find every legal and peaceful way around this conflict, our patience has worn thin.

Poor Rotch looked so frustrated when he finally did return at 5:45 this evening. Why did I really expect to receive a positive answer from the governor? Why should he begin to see our side now?

The Sons of Liberty have reached their boiling point. The citizens of these American colonies demand and deserve both their personal rights and their freedom from British rule. We are prospering settlers, ready to expand and govern ourselves.

The population of this country, in a few years will be more numerous than that of Great Britain and Ireland together. We have been branded as traitors and rebels only for complaining of our grievances. How long must this continue? We have had enough!

Thomas Hutchinson

Thursday, December 16, 1773

I have been here at my home in Milton now for two weeks. I wonder what would be happening in town now if I had chosen to stay in Boston? Escaping here was my only option to ensure my family's safety. I have done what I felt was best.

I am so very far away from England. Not having the necessary and official papers or instructions from the King, I had no other choice than to wait these patriots out and call their bluff. How can they challenge the power of Great Britain? Britain has given its colonists everything to begin their new lives here in the Americas. Without her financial help, wartime aid and supplies, and all the many imports over the past years, these colonists would have perished quickly. Why, I look around my home here and see that almost everything is a product from across the Atlantic in Great Britain, everything from the material in my cuff to the goblet in my cupboard, and the paper I am writing on. What would we do without Great Britain?

Then came the tea conflict. I acted as best I could under such confusion. So much seemed to happen so fast. I called the tea merchants together to try and discuss the tax situation, but none of them showed up. Without any official word from Great Britain, my hands were tied. I could not grant Quaker Rotch passage back to England without the taxes from his tea cargo. So he sits and waits. And I sit and wait.

Francis Rotch

Thursday, December 16, 1773

Today is the deadline. My ship, the Dartmouth, survived its eight-week long passage across the Atlantic from London, carrying one hundred-fourteen tea chests, only to be anchored offshore for two weeks in Boston harbor. I was the lead ship, leaving England a few days before the others. Since we have arrived, the Eleanor and the Beaver have also arrived with even more cargo of tea.

I rowed in when we arrived, expecting to be paid the taxes so that I could unload the tea and head back for England. I had wanted to get back before the cold winter months set in. Now, here I am, the captain of a ship full of sailors and tea, and I have no where to keep them but on the ship and have only limited food that is supposed to last us until we get back home. I had been planning to buy more food for our return trip after receiving payment for the cargo, but without payment, I cannot buy food.

What shall I do? My men are getting nervous, and so am I. The people have been calling meetings and talking about my ship. Why me? The patriots urged me to send the tea back without paying the tax. If I tried to unload the tea, my life would be in danger. There have been so many stories of tea merchants being tarred and feathered. I had thought them just fanciful stories. Now I know better. I could be one of them.

They sent me off today to seek permission for passage back to England from Governor Hutchinson. Seven miles in pouring rain I ran, hoping and praying that all would be resolved. But to no avail. The governor could not grant permission without authorization from Britain. Don't these people understand? All I want is to see my ship sail into the harbor, deposit its goods and return for more. It is my job.

I am a simple man, seeking a simple life. This is all too confusing for me. What do I do?

𝔅𝔬𝔰𝔱𝔬𝔫 𝔗𝔢𝔞 𝔓𝔞𝔯𝔱𝔶

What Really Happened

Old South Hall held over five thousand people inside its walls that wet and miserable day. Samuel Adams had sent Quaker Rotch to get permission for return passage home to England from the governor, but to no avail. Governor Hutchinson, living in his home seven miles away, had refused.

While awaiting this inevitable answer, Adams had already begun to plan the next move. While waiting for Rotch to return, over fifty volunteers were meeting at a friend's home, smearing paint or charcoal on their faces, draping blankets and torn jackets over themselves, trying to disguise themselves as Mohawk Indians.

At last Quaker Rotch arrived. The governor had refused passage. Adams gave the volunteers the sign to go ahead. The patriots would enact their plan.

The patriots marched down to the wharf carrying axes and knives. They split into three groups, each boarding one of the three ships carrying the tea. Upon boarding, the keys to the storage area were take from one of the ship's hands. All of the ship's men were then instructed to go below and remain quiet. Using their axes and knives, the patriots began chopping away at the chests of tea. Once opened, they grabbed the tea containers and threw them over the side of the ship into the sea.

A crowd had gathered along the wharf, but all were silent, almost in horror of all that was happening before their eyes.

After every bit of tea was thrown over the side, the disguised patriots marched back to their homes, exhilarated and proud. They had shown those Loyalists that they would not be intimidated any longer.

Samuel Adams wrote to his Committees of Correspondence, "We are in a perfect jubilee. Not a Tory in the whole community can find the least fault with our proceedings. The spirit of the people throughout the country is to be described by no terms in my power. Their conduct last night surprised the admiral and English gentlemen, who observed that these were not a mob of disorderly rabble, but men of sense, coolness and intrepidity."

Quaker Rotch, distraught and overwhelmed with the entire situation, headed back to England. What would he tell the tea commissioners in London? Possibly, he would have to return to his family in America as a farmer like all his other family members.

Governor Hutchinson was shocked at what the patriots had done. The harbor was a horrible display of splintered wood, tin containers and black tea. The patriots had won this battle. This was one of several incidents between England and the American colonies that led to the formation of the First Continental Congress in 1774 and eventually led to the Revolutionary War.

The Alamo
Background Information

The world was changing, with the most intense desire for change happening in the North American continent. British colonies in America had gained their independence; and Spain, who had controlled the Mexican territory since the 1700s, relinquished its power in 1821, granting Mexico its independence.

American Settlement in Texas

Many adventurous Americans sought their dream of land ownership in the Mexican territory known as Texas. One such adventurer, Stephen Austin, won a land grant of 200,000 acres to set up an American colony of 300 families in this western wilderness.

Austin and his party headed west in 1821 to the land they had been given between the Colorado and Brazo Rivers. During the next two years, the settlers worked hard to survive in the new land. The Mexican authorities were nervous, though. The Louisiana Purchase had created more westward movement than predicted, and many Americans had moved into the area in

such a short amount of time. Would the Americans try to take over Mexico someday too?

The Mexican Government

Mexico's government in 1824 was somewhat stable. It was a young government, and their constitution of 1824 guaranteed freedom to citizens under a democratic government. This was something new for Mexican citizens. The Mexican natives of Texas and the American settlers both enjoyed the constitution's freedoms. In return for this freedom, the settlers had to become Mexican citizens and take on the Catholic faith. The constitution also stated that when the population of Texas grew to a certain number, it would receive its own statehood under Mexico.

When the Mexican government decided in 1830 to give future American settlers protection from lawsuits and money troubles they may have had in the United

States, Americans swarmed to Texas. By 1832, over 30,000 Americans had settled in Texas. Some were hardworking like the first Americans who had come, but many were not. Some were corrupt, quick-tempered people who infuriated and embarrassed the Mexican officials, Mexican natives, and the earlier American settlers.

Meanwhile the Mexican government was in trouble. Democracy was not working. The United States, aware of the tensions brewing, offered to buy Texas from Mexico to ensure the rights of the Americans in Texas. The Mexican officials refused the offer, stopped further immigration altogether, and sent soldiers to enforce their decisions. The Mexican government had had enough of these Americans.

Santa Ana

The Mexican ruler at this time was El Presidente Santa Ana. Known for his fiery show of power and great confidence, Santa Ana took control of both the government and the army. Working loudly and harshly, he surmised that a government based on *tyranny* to be what Mexico needed at this time. They could not live under this so-called *democracy*. He would have to be tough at first, giving his people little freedom, but they would eventually regain their pride and status with Santa Ana in charge.

A Request for Statehood

A famous Indian scout and congressman by the name of Sam Houston, a big, rough-and-tumble sort of a man, had found his way to Texas. He had been there for only four months when he was elected to represent the people of Texas at an American convention in April of 1833. At the convention Sam Houston wrote Texas's first Constitution and decided that Austin needed to talk with the Mexican officials in Mexico City about granting Texas its independence.

In July of 1833, Austin traveled to Mexico City to discuss this option with Santa Ana, confident there were enough people in Texas now to validate statehood.

Instead of being granting statehood, Austin was arrested and put in jail for 18 months. When he returned home in July of 1835, he told the people of Texas that their "only choice is war!"

The call for freedom for Texas had reached far across the United States. Soldiers, volunteers and heroic leaders such as Jim Bowie, Buck Travis and Davy Crockett heard of the Americans' fight for freedom against Santa Ana.

A Battle with Santa Ana

Houston was appointed Commander-in-Chief of the Texan army. Santa Ana sent his troops into Texas to patrol the borders. The Texans were angered. Many native Texans of Mexican descent were horrified at the thought of having a ruler treat them so badly. Others, scared of Santa Ana, quickly joined the Mexican troops. The Americans were not used to being under the control of another country's dictator and were anxious to do something about the situation.

Houston warned them. "Wait for the cannon to arrive. Take time to drill the men", he commanded. "Better do well late than never."

50

They could not wait. The first shots rang out on October 2, 1835 when 100 Mexican troops from San Antonio rode into the town of Gonzales and demanded the Texans turn over their cannon located in the center of town. Almaron Dickinson, in charge of the artillery, held fast to his cannon. The Texans, eager to fight, charged the soldiers, opened fire and killed one Mexican. The other Mexican troops retreated.

The Conflict Escalates

Santa Ana was furious when he heard the news of spilled Mexican blood on Mexican land.

"I shall grind them into the dust!" he shouted.

Austin traveled to Washington to ask for support from the United States, while James Neill and Bowie took over the anxious Texan troops now in San Antonio, facing a stand off with 400 Mexican soldiers. How long could the standoff last?

The men finally could wait no longer. On December 5, 1835, the Texans took San Antonio in a brutal five-day siege. Soldiers went from street to street, house to house until finally the Mexicans surrendered. They were sent back to Mexico with a promise never to fight Texas again. All of Texas began to celebrate.

Houston wasn't ready to celebrate, though. He knew it wasn't over yet. Santa Ana would come back. He didn't think Santa Ana would risk marching across the barren lands during the dead of winter though, so he decided to go north in search of help from the Indians. To be on the safe side, Houston sent orders for Captain Neill to take the cannon out and blow up the Alamo. He felt that during a battle anyone inside the fort would be trapped. The officials in San Antonio, however, disregarded Houston's order and set up a soldier's camp in the fort instead.

The Alamo

Christmas had come and gone, as well as the New Year. The year was 1836. Bowie was worried about the shortages of troops, provisions and ammunitions. There weren't enough Texans to protect the entire city. They would have to go to the Alamo and defend the Texans from this small fortress.

On February 11 Colonel Buck Travis arrived with 26 men and some much needed supplies. Colonel Davy Crockett followed with twelve volunteers from Tennessee. The grand total of Texan soldiers in San Antonio then was 180. Travis took command of the troops and moved them into the Alamo. He felt confident that Houston would return soon with more troops and that they would be fine in the meantime.

Meanwhile, Santa Ana had heard of the disaster in San Antonio. Who did these Americans think they were? How dare they defy their ruler? They were in Mexico, not America. Santa Ana felt that he had to do something.

Santa Ana Returns

No one expected to see Santa Ana until spring, but on February 23, 1836, Santa Ana arrived with over 1,000 lancers, followed by 6,000 infantrymen and artillery. Against all odds he had taken 7,500 Mexican soldiers across 150 miles of barren wasteland in the dead of winter.

Travis and Bowie rang the bell warning of Santa Ana's coming. All the soldiers of the Texan army took refuge inside the walls of the Alamo. Besides the American troops, there were seven Mexican natives including Gregorio Esparza and his family, a few Mexican women, and Susanna Dickinson and her daughter.

Santa Ana would allow them one last chance to surrender. He waved a bright red flag on top of one of the buildings in town. The red flag meant, "No mercy to men who don't surrender." Santa Ana waited for a response.

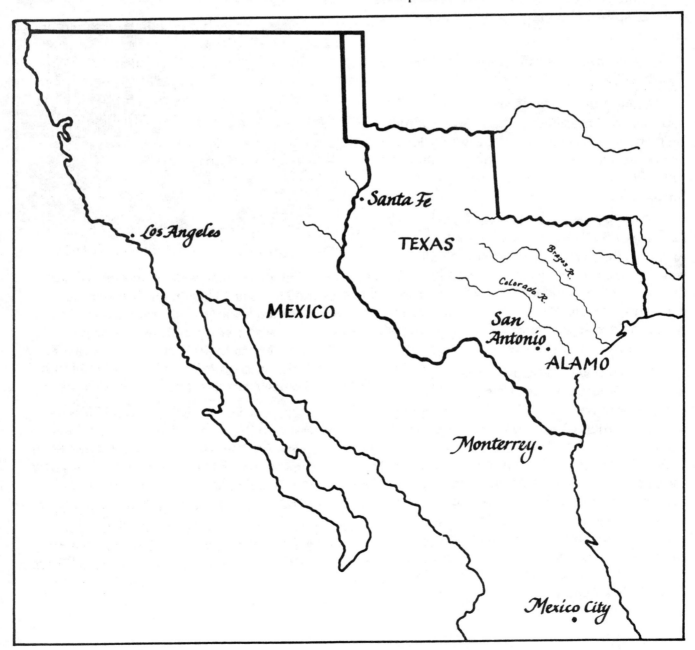

52

Gregorio Esparza

Gregorio Esparza was a native Texan. He was born on March 8, 1808 in the town of San Antonio. He married another Texas native named Ana Salazar.

Ana had a daughter from her first marriage. After they married, Ana and Gregorio had three sons of their own, Enrique, Gregorio, and Manuel.

Gregorio and Ana were very happy with their family and home, yet were becoming greatly troubled by the uneasiness of their fellow Texans. Santa Ana was not treating the Texans fairly. He felt there were too many Americans in Texas, and he was treating everyone in Texas with the same cruelty that he intended for the Americans.

The Americans that Gregorio knew were good, hard-working people. He liked the settlers' ways, their independent thinking and their talk of *democracy*. He had been hopeful, as were the Americans, that Texas would soon be given its statehood; but Santa Ana had trampled these dreams. Gregorio would fight for justice. He joined the company of native Texans, the Texas Volunteers, in 1835.

Gregorio's brother, Francisco, was also a native Texan, yet he did not share the same beliefs as his brother Gregorio. Francisco felt a closer tie to Mexico than did Gregorio. He felt Texas needed to follow the ruling government out of loyalty and respect for their ancestors. Most importantly, however, Francisco knew that Santa Ana was not someone you wanted to anger. Truly, Francisco felt the way he did out of fear of Santa Ana who would kill anyone who stood in the way of his power.

Gregorio looked at each of his neighbors, wondering if they too would run in fear with Santa Ana's men or stay and fight for Texas and its independence.

Winter was coming. The weather was getting colder. The Mexican army was coming to San Antonio. Gregorio came home and told Ana to stay well-hidden from the fighting that was going to come and to protect the children. He chose to fight – against Santa Ana, against his brother, but for Texan independence.

Sam Houston

Sam Houston was a giant of a man whose confidence and desire for power and honor have made him a famous American hero.

The youngest of five boys, Sam moved through his childhood quickly. He read books constantly, especially books about heroes, and longed for excitement and adventure. At 14 years of age, he ran away to live with the most exciting people he had heard about, the Cherokee Indians. He was adopted by the chief, given the name Raven, and lived as an Indian for three years.

After he returned to his home town, he joined the U.S. Army at the age of 20. His mother gave him a ring he would wear for the rest of his life. It was inscribed with the single word "honor." Houston took this word to heart as he vowed always to follow his quest for things that were bigger and better to make his family proud.

By 1832, at the age of 39, Houston had been an Indian Scout, a soldier, a U.S. Congressman, and governor of Tennessee. When his governorship was over, he was in search of something new and exciting. He found this new challenge in Texas.

Houston became a Mexican citizen and joined the Catholic Church. Four months later, Texans elected him to office. He went on to write the first constitution of the young government. Houston was proud of his work but was becoming more and more disappointed with the people he represented. These Texans were impatient, noisy, and rude. How could he inspire these Texans to follow his wise words?

When tensions flared with Mexico's El Presidente Santa Ana over the Texans' desire for independence, the temporary government of Texas appointed Houston Major General of the army. Houston warned the Texans not to rush into a war with Mexico. They needed to organize themselves, to wait for cannons to arrive from the states, and to drill the men.

"Better do well late than never," he proclaimed to the men. He knew success would only come after things had been prepared and set into place. How could he get these Texans to understand this? Houston knew he would have to do something to resolve this crisis.

Santa Ana

Antonio Lopez de Santa Ana was born in Jalapa, Mexico, on February 21, 1794. His father was a Spaniard, his mother of Mexican descent. They were a poor, yet proud family. Santa Ana went to school until he was 14, then his life began to change.

Santa Ana had always been a high-spirited and active child. He was a natural-born leader who showed great confidence in all that he did. His parents were told their son needed more schooling and agreed to send him away to live with General Davila. The general felt "his vaulting ambition" would make him a true leader of Mexico someday.

Santa Ana enjoyed the military life. He fought under Davila in the quest for Mexican independence from Spain. In time he turned against Davila, his father-figure for 13 years, and at the age of 27, began paving his own pathway to the Mexican presidency. He fought on both sides of Mexico's problems, depending on who had the greatest power at that time. He supported a ruler one day, and led others to overthrow him the next.

In 1833, this boastful and fiery fellow rose to the title of El Presidente of Mexico. He was married, had 3 children, and became known as the Napoleon of the West. He thrived on the attention and power.

"El Presidente Santa Ana has the bearing of an Emperor; and when he goes about in public, escorted by fifty hussars in plumed helmets and burnished breastplates, riding a powerful black stallion, one is deafened by the 'vivas' of the crowds . . . Everything about the 'Napoleon of the West' – from the gold-hilted sword he wears, to his gold-embossed saddle with a horn shaped like an eagle gives the impression of a person is to be reckoned with," an admiring British visitor to Mexico City wrote in a letter home.

Santa Ana would not be pushed around by these Texans who continued to disobey and dishonor him. These "Yanquis" would be taught a lesson!

Susanna Dickinson

Susanna grew up in Tennessee. At the age of 15, she married Almaron Dickinson. The young couple headed west to the Mexican-ruled Texas. They arrived at DeWitt's colony on May 5, 1834 and settled in the town of Gonzales. The Dickinsons were granted town lots, thus beginning their exciting, yet dangerous life on the wild frontier.

Almaron became a skilled blacksmith, especially when it came to working with guns. Susanna took care of the everyday chores needed to survive on the frontier. She made their first home as pleasant as she could.

In December 1834, Susanna and Almaron became proud parents of a baby girl named Angelina, and Almaron was appointed commissioner of the area. Susanna couldn't have been more proud. She had a strong, loving husband, a beautiful baby girl, and a home and future in the soon-to-be state of Texas.

Less than a year later, life in Texas began to change. Santa Ana had taken control of the government in Texas.

Almaron was anxious. He had been appointed lieutenant, to be in charge of the Texas Volunteer Army's artillery. He knew he would eventually have to fight Santa Ana's army.

Almaron and his family joined Austin and the volunteers as they marched off to San Antonio. Almaron was appointed Captain of Artillery. Susanna and Almaron were invited to come live with the Mexican Governor of Texas and his wife. Susanna prepared the meals and cleaned the clothes while Almaron met with the volunteer army to discuss options.

The Alamo

Investigator Questions

The following are questions you may use in questioning the Who's Who team members. Add some questions of your own, being careful to be unbiased and to allow each side of the story to be shared.

Questions for Susanna Dickinson, Texas frontierswoman

1. You and your husband did not want to continue living in Tennessee after your were married. Where did you move and why?

2. Upon arriving in Gonzales, you and Almaron became Mexican citizens. Why?

3. At Christmas, in 1834, you were a very proud and confident young woman. Why was that?

4. Explain to us how you felt when the warning bell rang announcing Santa Ana's arrival. What do you think of him?

Ask your own questions.

_____

_____

_____

Questions for El Presidente Santa Ana, ruler of Mexico

1. Your childhood was different from most boys in Mexico. Why was that?

2. Mexico won its independence from Spain in 1823. For 7 years the rulers of Mexico have tried to build a democratic government. You have different ideas. What are they?

3. You are angered at the Americans who have come to Texas. Why? What are your reasons for wanting them out of your land after the Mexican government had originally welcomed them?

4. Why did you give the Texans a chance to surrender when you reached San Antonio and knew they were in the Alamo?

Ask your own questions.

_____

_____

_____

Alamo Questions, Continued

Questions for Sam Houston, Texas Representative

1. Why did you send Stephen Austin to Mexico City in April of 1833?

2. What happened when Santa Ana's men came to the town of Gonzales? Did you support what happened?

3. Where were you and what were you doing when Santa Ana arrived in San Antonio?

4. Why did you feel it was safe to leave San Antonio and travel north?

Ask your own questions.

_____

_____

_____

_____

Questions for Gregorio Esparza, native of Mexico

1. Why did you join the Texas Volunteer Army?

2. The American settlers who have come to Texas have become your friends. What did you see in them that others, including your brother, did not?

3. How did you and your brother differ in your views concerning Santa Ana and politics?

4. As a father and a husband, what were some of the things you were worried about when you heard Santa Ana might come to San Antonio?

Ask your own questions.

_____

_____

_____

_____

Gregorio Esparza

February 23, 1834

I remember the day I joined the American Army. I had such hatred for El Presidente Santa Ana. His laws were so unfair. Life had become so miserable. Texas had had enough! We would stand up to Santa Ana and fight for our independence. I would not let Santa Ana take away everything my family and I had worked for.

How could I ask my dear Ana and our four children to stay here with me and this army of defenders? There were rumors that Santa Ana was on his way here to San Antonio. Should I leave with the others or stay?

My compadre gave me a wagon and food to take my family away from here, but it was too late. Santa Ana came today. If I stayed in town, I would have to fight against the Volunteers. I thought of finding Francisco and having Ana and the children stay with him, but we were too late. We would all have to hide in the Alamo with the rest of the Volunteers.

It took us all day to move to the Alamo. We got here just before dark. All of the doors were closed and barred shut. We went to the side where the church was. It was closed, but we crawled through a window, over a cannon, and then quickly closed the window behind us. My family was finally safe.

I have been given an 18 pound cannon to tend, and I will do so with all my strength. I have placed the cannon close to the chapel where my dear Ana prays to God that all this will soon end in peace.

Diary Entry

Sam Houston

February 23, 1836

Rain . . . rain . . . rain.

The skies continue to shed torrents of rain on us. How many more nights will we have to roll out our blankets onto the wet ground?

I left San Antonio in search of Cherokee Chief Bowles, one of my closest friends, on my way to attend the March 1st convention in Washington-on-the-Brazo. This eastern part of Texas is so vast. I can see for miles. I hoped to talk to the Chief Bowles to make sure that the Cherokees and their 12 bands would support Texans in a war. We all have a lot to gain by working together.

The convention starts in a few days. There, we will build a future for Texas, first on paper and then in manpower and strategy.

I think of Travis, Bowie and Crockett back in San Antonio. Such experience and military strength I have never seen in one place. I feel confident they can hold the town until Santa Ana's return in the spring.

Having given orders to demolish the Alamo makes me feel at ease. Anyone caught inside there during an ambush would be doomed. They would be trapped and unable to protect themselves.

How could Santa Ana not regard Texas as anything but a grand land awaiting its statehood? How dare he go against the Mexican constitution and the promise of statehood?

I am anxious to create this new Texas at the convention. Only days away from celebrating my 43rd birthday, I feel this young Texas is to be my greatest accomplishment. We are one, Texas and I.

Diary Entry

Santa Ana

February 23, 1836

Viva la Mexico!

I have seen Mexico through many changes and hard times over my 42 years. I have seen its rise to independence from Spain and a succession of leaders, each struggling to build a democratic government they knew nothing about. I have supported and overthrown all of them in my rise to ruler of all of Mexico.

These Americans in Texas are causing a lot of strife. There are too many of them — over 30,000 Americans have settled here in only a few short years. They are taking over my land. They are loud, obnoxious leeches. I want them out!

I have sacrificed a lot to come here to San Antonio in the dead of winter; but these Americans angered me so after capturing this town, I just had to come and face them myself. I knew my men would march without question. They know I am ruler.

We have arrived in San Antonio. I have over 7,000 men. Our cannons are ready to blow off every rooftop within the presidio. These petty survivors seeking safety in the Alamo will not last forever.

I will offer them life for their surrender, but these pompous, Americans will probably not choose wisely. My men are thirsty for blood, and they shall be satisfied in due time.

Texas is big, but I am bigger. I will teach these Americans to stay in their own land. They do not need to be on my land any longer. They have their United States and that is where they should be!

Diary Entry

Susanna Dickinson

February 23, 1836

Last night was a happy time. Davy had been itching to kick up some dust with his fiddle, and when he sauntered in last night over at Travis', everyone welcomed him and his Tennessee tunes. Almaron took my hand and spun me as if we were still courting. Travis' slave, Joe, clapped his hands and tapped his toes to the beat, smiling from ear to ear. Yes, it was a happy moment inside these thick fortress walls.

Travis shared in the beauty of our time together by giving our little Angelina a gift I shall always cherish. He removed a cat's eye ring from his finger, knotted it onto a string, and then placed it around Angelina's neck. For a fleeting moment, we forgot where we were.

Only yesterday, Senora Musquiz and I had been planning the day's meals together when we heard the bells of San Fernando ring out in a warning. We ran outside to see what had happened.

The Mexican army was coming!

Suddenly, Almaron rode up to the adobe and called to me to go with him to the Alamo. I mounted the bare back of his horse, sitting behind his saddle, holding Angelina close. The Alamo would protect us, I thought.

Once inside, I found I was the only white woman here. It does not matter. We are strong, all of us. I look into the eyes of the few Mexican women and children and see the same hope and desperation I know they see in my eyes.

Almaron says El Presidente started this war. All I know is that he took away my home, my friends, and my freedom. A chill has just shuddered up my spine. Will Santa Ana also take away my family?

The Alamo

What Really Happened

Santa Ana waved a bright red flag for all to see. This gesture meant, "No mercy to men who don't surrender." Then he and his 7,500 men waited for a response.

Travis sent Colonel Fannin in Goliad a letter asking for help. Fannin, not wanting to react too quickly and possibly endanger his troops, decided to wait before he responded. Travis sent another letter north to Washington-on-the-Brazo where the March 1st Convention was going to be held only five days later. Houston rode into the city the same night the letter arrived.

The letter was addressed to the people of Texas and all Americans in the world and said, "I will never surrender or retreat . . . Victory or Death!"

Houston knew that Fannin and his troops would be on their way to the Alamo, so he decided to stay for the convention before heading out to battle.

The convention began the next day. The Texans would first write a Declaration of Independence, putting on paper the freedoms they were fighting for. Huddled inside the only wood-floored building in the town, the men wrote and signed the declaration on March second.

By March 5th the fighting in San Antonio had been going on for 12 days. The Texans had not lost one soldier. Crockett and his volunteers lived up to their reputation by killing scores of Mexican soldiers.

Word came from Fannin that he would not be sending his troops to help wage war against Santa Ana. Travis was on his own. He collected all his troops and drew a line in the sand.

"Those who would stay and fight to the death, step over this mark. The others may leave with our thanks for sticking so long." Travis said.

All the men stepped over the line except one, says the legend. Even Bowie, ill with pneumonia, had his men carry him over the line. Susanna Dickinson and Ana Esparza watched as their husbands crossed over the line.

The end came on March 6, 1836. The massacre began before dawn with a sea of bugles blaring.

"We could hear the Mexican officers shouting to the men to jump over," said Enrique Esparza, Gregorio's 8 year old son, "and the men were fighting so close that we could near them strike each other. If was so dark that we couldn't see anything."

The women and children were all huddled in the southeast corner of the church in a small room to the right of the entrance doors.

"Finally," Enrique continues, "they began shooting through the dark into the room where we were. A boy who was wrapped in a blanket in one corner was hit and killed. The Mexicans fired into the room for at least fifteen minutes. It was a miracle but none of us children were touched."

"By daybreak the firing had almost stopped, and through the window we could see shadows of men moving around inside the fort. The Mexicans went from room to room looking for an American to kill," he states. All 188 Alamo defenders were dead.

Another survivor, the only Anglo woman in the fortress, Susanna Dickinson, continued the story by saying that she "took her babe in her arms and a pitcher of water, and visited the bleeding soldiers." She saw the faces of Travis, Bowie, Bonham and Crockett, all dead. But not Almaron's.

Discovered by Santa Ana's nephew, Almonte, she was told to follow him to his uncle's tent. On the way, she was grazed in the leg by a flying bullet and was taken to a hospital instead.

Meanwhile, Santa Ana met with all of the women and children in the Alamo. He gave each of the women two dollars and a blanket and told them they were free to go where they wanted. Ana Esparza took her children to Francisco's home. Francisco had received permission to remove his brother's body and give him a proper burial. His was the only burial, however. Santa Ana had ordered the bodies of the Texans to be piled in heaps and burned, the final insult.

Looking out into the heavy smoke of death, Susanna prepared to meet Santa Ana. He paraded around her proudly, flaunting his power and majesty. He paid extra attention to Angelina and even offered to adopt her. Susanna refused him defiantly. When Santa Ana became aware that his charm and power was not impressing this woman, he ordered her and her child sent back to Gonzales.

On March 8th Susanna and her daughter left San Antonio on horseback. They met Joe, Travis' slave, and traveled together. Five days later they spotted three men who were Houston's scouts who had been sent out to determine Travis' situation at the Alamo. They helped Susanna, Joe and Angelina get to Gonzales. There Susanna told her friends, many of them wives and mothers of men at the Alamo, that all of the men at the Alamo, including Almaron, had been killed.

Houston was in Gonzales, too. He listened to her every word. When he learned that Santa Ana had burned the bodies of the Texans, he flew into a rage and vowed revenge.

Santa Ana was still in San Antonio with his army, planning greater Texan conquests. Two and a half weeks after the battle at the Alamo he came upon Fannin and his men in Goliad. Instead of fighting, the 393 Texans surrendered, expecting to be taken as prisoners. Instead, Santa Ana lined them up and shot them.

Houston knew at this point that he was Texas' last hope for independence. Houston planned his strategies carefully, running ahead of Santa Ana and making him chase him, hoping he would leave some of his troops behind during the pursuit.

Then, on April 21, near Buffalo Bayou and the San Jacinto River, Santa Ana finally met his match. There, Houston and 783 Texans surprised Santa Ana and his 1,500 men. Blocking all escape routes, the Texans pounced on the Mexicans shouting "Remember the Alamo! Remember Goliad!"

Less than 20 minutes later, the napping Santa Ana awoke to find 630 of his men killed and the rest taken prisoner. Only 9 Texans had died. Texas was free!

Fugitive Slave Law
Background Information

The story begins during the 1500s in the vast New World. The characters in the story are the curious and adventurous Europeans who had just discovered the Americas. To make the land profitable, they would need a large supply of cheap labor. They found what they needed in West Africa. The Europeans took the West Africans from their homes and sold them into slavery in the New World.

Slavery Is Legalized

In 1640 three indentured servants in Virginia, ran away from their master. One was a Dutchman, one was a Scot, (both had been indentured servants because of a crime they had committed), and one was an African named John Punch. The three were captured in Maryland and returned to their owners. As punishment, the Virginia court decided the Dutchman and the Scot would have four more years added to their time as servants. John Punch got a different sentence. He was ordered to serve his master "for the time of his natural life." He was made a slave.

Within a year, the Massachusetts colony recognized slavery by law by stating that slavery was forbidden except in the case of "lawful captives taken in just wars" (like the Indians) and "strangers. . . sold to us" (like the African

strangers brought over by the slave trade. In other words, Slavery was *legalized*.

Anti-Slavery Feelings

About one hundred years later, in 1750, the Quakers took a stand against slavery. This was the first group who voiced their feelings on *human rights* in opposition to the government. By 1790, more people opposed slavery, especially in the North where there weren't as many slaves. The population totals told a story in themselves. In Massachusetts the slave population was a mere 1.4%, New York's was 7.6%, while South Carolina had a 43% slave population.

1793 was an important year for the slavery issue for two reasons. One reason was the passage of an act that basically made slavery a racial issue. The act stated that peoples of color were property and were directed by law to comply with the owner's wishes. All those who ran away were to be returned to their owners. The second reason was the invention of the cotton gin that allowed the plantation owners of the South to expand their fields of cotton, which ultimately created the need for more slave labor.

Fifteen years later, in 1808, America forbade their ships to engage in the slave trade. The importation of slaves was now illegal in America. There would be no more slaves brought into the United States, yet that would not stop the slave owners of the South from needing more children to be born into slavery to guarantee a future work force.

The Great Compromiser

A main character in the story is Henry Clay. Born in Virginia in 1777, he grew up as America was maturing as a nation. Clay's legal life had led him to become Kentucky's representative in Congress and eventually the Speaker of the House.

Clay's strength showed itself clearly in 1820. Missouri and Maine both wanted statehood. There was debate about admitting a state that held so many slaves within its boundaries. Missouri had over 2,500 slaves. Clay tried to make everyone happy by creating the *Missouri Compromise*, which stated that after the admission of Maine and Missouri, all future states in areas north of 36 °30' N latitude would enter as free states, and all others south of the line would enter as slave states. Thus, Maine entered as a free state, and Missouri entered as a slave state. This act clearly made the distinction between the industrial North and the agricultural South.

Three Slaves

Three additional characters enter the story; all slaves, one from a northern state and two from a southern state. Frederick Douglass was born in 1816 in Maryland. His mother was

a black slave and his father was white. Frederick knew neither of his parents and was raised by his grandmother until he was sold at the age of 8 years.

The southern state of Georgia was the birthplace of two slaves named William and Ellen. William Craft was born in 1823. He had a close family, but their life on the plantation was harsh.

Ellen, was born three years later in 1826. Her mother was a slave, but her father was her mother's white slave owner. Ellen's complexion was very fair, but since Ellen's mother was a slave, she was a slave as well.

Growing Tension

The United States was a growing country. The 1830 census showed a total of 12,866,020 Americans. Following the cotton gin, invention of the the locomotive and the steam engine encouraged the push for more expansion and growth.

Not everyone saw the same dream, however. Southern slave-owning states started worrying about all this westward expansion. Would slavery spread or would the politicians from the North not allow it? Southerners reasoned that slavery was a national benefit and not a national evil as the northerners claimed it to be. The southern states began to talk about withdrawing from the Union.

All this controversy started everyone thinking, including the slaves. On August 21, 1831, Nat Turner led his followers on a slave revolt. Sixty whites were killed, and over 140 blacks were killed. From that day on, southern slave masters became more cautious and strict, and the abolitionists in the north became more angry and convinced that slavery was wrong.

Slavery and escaped fugitives had become a major issue. Frederick Douglass had escaped to Massachusetts and wrote his autobiography in 1845, which sold more than 30,000 copies in the following five years. In the midst of it all; however, life for the slaves went on as usual. For the most part, the slaves were kept unaware of all that was going on with the fight against slavery.

Two years later, on September 14, 1847, the Mexican War ended. The United States acquired land from Texas to California and north to Oregon; 3 million square miles. What would happen to all this land? So much of it was below the 36° 30' line. Would the Missouri Compromise be enacted or would the people in each state decide individually whether they wanted to be a free or slave state?

Then gold was discovered in California, and in less than a year, there were over 100,000 '49ers seeking their fortunes in California.

An Escape

Slaves' escapes to freedom were increasing steadily. Always dreaming of their freedom, as well, William and Ellen thought of a plan to escape from their slave owners into the promised land, the North. They spent days planning and preparing, and on Wednesday, December 21, 1848, they began their escape.

Ellen, having a white complexion, dressed as a sickly Southern gentleman traveling with his slave (William). They boarded the train in Macon, Georgia and headed north. Ellen, portraying a fictitious Mr. Johnson, pretended to be deaf so she wouldn't have to speak to anyone. Her disguise was a success on the first day.

During the next few days Ellen and William had many close calls, but finally on Christmas morning, they arrived together in Philadelphia. Their escape worked! Because Philadelphia was too close to the border for them to be completely safe, they were advised to travel farther north to Boston.

Upon arriving in Boston, they met some abolitionist friends who helped them find a home and work. One important friend was Reverend Theodore Parker. He introduced them to Frederick Douglass and other key abolitionists in town.

$100 REWARD!
RUNAWAY

from subscriber, Macon Georgia on the 21st of December, 1848. A negro man known as William about 24 years old, weighs about 150 pounds, scar on left forearm.

The above reward will be given to any person who may apprehend this said runaway negro.

William Hughes

Feeling settled, William and Ellen attended an abolition meeting. They were so thankful for their own freedom, but knowing their families and friends were still in slavery was extremely disheartening. They told their escape story in hopes that the movement would continue to bring about freedom for all those in slavery.

Unbeknownst to William and Ellen, their speech found its way into a Charleston newspaper, which then was reprinted in the Macon weekly, so their owners found out where they were.

Clay's Compromise

Tensions were rising in Washington, D.C. Sentiment in favor of disunion was at its peak now, and Clay was trying desperately to work out a compromise to keep everyone happy and most importantly, keep the Union together. Clay, known now as the Great Compromiser, came up with the following plan.

1. California would be allowed to enter as a free state; the remaining land in the West could choose to be either slave or free.

Texas would break itself up into smaller states to form several slave states, and the United States would take care of all its debts.

3. Slave trading would be outlawed in Washington D.C., but slavery would still continue.

(The first three of these provisions were equally balanced for both the slave and the free states. The last one was not.)

The Fugitive Slave Law

4. Congress was not to interfere with interstate slave trade. Instead, the states would appoint local commissioners to resolve slave ownership conflicts. All that was needed to retrieve an escaped slave was a written notice from the slave owner. There would be no jury trial, only a decision by the commissioner. Each commissioner would be paid $10.00 for every slave returned and $5.00 if he only reviewed the case.

Heavy debate rattled through Washington over the Compromise. President Fillmore, while opposing slavery, saw no other option to save the Union than to sign Clay's Compromise and put the Fugitive Slave Law into action. He signed it on September 18, 1850.

By September 21, 40 Negroes had left the once safe town of Boston. Fillmore sent troops to both the North and the South to stifle uprisings. The land was in an uproar.

The Visitor

On a Monday morning in October, William Craft had a visitor in the cabinet shop. It was John Knight, a white man he had worked with in Macon's cabinet shop. He wanted William to show him the town. What he really wanted was to have William step out of the shop and into the hands of a slave hunter William knew was accompanying Knight. William dared not go.

Knight came back the following day, too. He urged William to bring Ellen to his hotel that night so she could hear stories of her mother. Ellen and William stayed in their home, scared to go to sleep.

Wednesday brought a message from Knight that he was to leave on Thursday and that if either one of them wanted to send any messages home to their families, they had better bring them to his hotel that evening. Ellen and William were frightened. Would they be robbed of their hopes and dreams by these white men? They vowed they would rather die than go back to bondage.

They ran to tell Reverend Parker of their problem. He took Ellen to a friend's house for safe hiding and told William to stand ready at his home, armed.

Meanwhile, Parker and abolitionist friends spotted Knight with a slave jailer from Macon, William Hughes. They had come to deliver William and Ellen back to their owners. These slaves had no rights and no government to help them. They were legally the property of two white men.

Henry Clay

Henry Clay was born on April 12, 1777 in Hanover County, Virginia. Raised in a moderately well-to-do home, Clay was destined for political life. He studied law and entered the bar at the age of 20 in 1797. Hearing that there were plenty of land title disputes in the expansion area, Clay moved to Kentucky. His high energy, ambitious yet sensitive manner, and tremendous speaking abilities led him into politics quickly. He soon became involved in writing the state's constitution. He became Kentucky's representative in Congress and served as Speaker of the House.

Clay despised slavery and wanted Kentucky to grant emancipation to all its slaves. After spending time in the government, however, he found that seeking emancipation was a lost cause and thus accepted the ideas of slave ownership on a national scale. He did, however, provide for his own slaves' freedom in his will.

As the industrial North clashed with the agrarian South, some states began talking about breaking away from the Union. Clay could not let the union fall apart. His Missouri Compromise allowed Missouri to enter the union as a slave state, allowed Maine to enter as a free state, and established a line for future decisions about whether a state would allow slavery or not. Clay had eased the tensions for a short time.

By 1850, the United States had acquired over four times the amount of land they had had when Clay was born. Slavery continued to be a hotly debated topic, with North and South on opposite sides and the South continuing to talk about secession. Clay began to search out a compromise – anything to settle the fears of those who wanted to break away from the Union.

His Compromise of 1850 passed. The Great Compromiser had managed to ward off the inevitable clash of the North versus the South for the time being.

Ellen Craft

Ellen was born in a wealthy slave owner's home in Macon, Georgia in 1826. When little Ellen was born with white skin, the mistress swore to make Ellen's life miserable, because she was the daughter of her husband and a slave woman. For eleven years, Ellen endured harsh scolding and abuse.

The mistress of the house always resented Ellen, so when her daughter, Eliza, was going to get married, it was decided that Ellen would be given to the married couple as a wedding gift. Her new mistress was kind to her, but Ellen continued to feel sad and angry about everything that had happened to her. She felt like a thing, not a person with feelings and ideas.

Then she met a young slave named William when she was seventeen. Two years later Ellen and William were married. Ellen and William worked long, hard days, Ellen in the mansion and William in the cabinet shop. William, a skilled craftsman, began receiving a small percentage of the price of each piece of work he finished.

Ellen would hear her owners talking about runaway slaves sometimes. William heard stories, too. He heard of one slave who had packaged himself in a box and mailed himself to Philadelphia from Richmond, Virginia. He was hungry and weak when he arrived, but he made it. He was free!

Most of the runaway slaves got caught and were beaten in front of all the other slaves so no one else would try to run away. Somehow it just made Ellen and William desire their freedom even more. They were always thinking of a plan that would work.

A week before Christmas in 1848, William thought of the incredible plan that would take them from Macon to Philadelphia and freedom. Ellen would dress up as a sickly young gentleman from the South who was traveling with his slave. They both received traveling passes to visit an elderly aunt a few miles away. Finally, on December 21, they boarded the train to leave Macon. Their journey toward freedom had begun.

William Hughes

Little is known about William Hughes other than his name, job title, and his participation in the lives of Ellen and William Craft. Therefore, much of what is written below has been compiled from various slave recordings concerning those who had the job of tracking down and delivering fugitive slaves.

William Hughes was born in Macon, Georgia. His father worked for one of the plantations as a slave overseer. William grew up believing that slaves were of little human value. They were the property of the slave owners. When William was a teenager, he'd go over to the plantation and with the owner's sons would taunt and ridicule the slaves. He knew that whites could do anything they wanted with the slaves. It was their right. He hated slaves. He felt superior to them in every way.

In time William followed in his father's footsteps, working on another plantation overseeing slaves, until he was appointed to work in town at the county jail. He liked all the attention he got while working in the jail.

Once the Fugitive Slave Law was passed it became easier to bring back runaway slaves. The abolitionists would have to pay a fine of $1,000 and spend six months in jail if they got involved in the escape of a fugitive slave. Slaves could be brought in without having to go through any legal process and without a warrant. William felt that was the way it should have been all along.

One hot September day, Dr. Collins and Mr. Taylor, two very respected and wealthy men in the town, came to the county jail. They had a young carpenter, John Knight, with them. They brought with them an article from the newspaper, featuring a story of two runaway slaves by the name of Craft. The two owners wanted the return of their slaves. William was chosen to go to Boston and return them to their owners. Mr. Knight would go with him to provide proof that they were bringing back the right people.

Frederick Douglass

Frederick Douglass was truly the most powerful slave to join the abolition movement and became the first black citizen to hold a high-ranking position in the United States government.

Born to a slave mother and white father in 1817 in Maryland, Frederick Augustus Washington Bailey never knew either of his parents. He was raised by his grandmother on a Maryland plantation. At the age of eight years, Frederick was sold to a family in Baltimore as a house servant. Though it was against the law, his mistress began teaching him how to read. When the master of the house stopped the lessons, Frederick continued to learn on his own.

Frederick was 16 years old when his master died. He was first sent to work in the fields and then to work in the shipyards. At the age of 21 he disguised himself as a sailor and escaped to New York City. From there, he traveled to New Bedford, Massachusetts, changed his name to Douglass and began working as a laborer.

While attending an anti-slavery convention in 1841, he was asked to share his experiences and feelings about slavery. His speech was intense and powerful. He was immediately enlisted as an agent for the Massachusetts Anti-Slavery Society.

He went on to write his autobiography in 1845 and then left the United States and went to England for two years to avoid being recaptured by his former owner whom he had talked about in his book. He returned in 1847 with money for both his freedom and his own anti-slavery newspaper, the *North Star*, which was published from 1847 to 1860.

Receiving total support and respect from the abolition crowds, he rarely received acceptance from the general public. During his speeches he was often assaulted with catcalls, firecrackers and rotten food. The abolitionists were planning to meet and discuss the Fugitive Slave Law. He would make it clear to the people of Boston that they must take a stand on injustices against Negroes, even if it meant going against the government.

Fugitive Slave Law

Investigator Questions

The following are questions you may use in questioning the Who's Who team members. Add some questions of your own, being careful to be unbiased and to allow each side of the story to be shared.

Questions for Ellen Craft, fugitive slave

1. What was your childhood like?

2. How did you and William escape from Macon?

3. What was your life in Boston like?

4. If given the chance, what would you like to say to Mr. Knight and Mr. Hughes?

Ask your own questions.

_____

_____

_____

_____

Questions for Henry Clay, the Great Compromiser

1. How did you earn the title of the Great Compromiser?

2. What are your personal feelings about slavery? How does it affect your role as a government official?

3. What were your reasons for creating the Compromise of 1850?

4. Explain the Fugitive Slave Law.

Ask your own questions.

_____

_____

_____

_____

Fugitive Slave Law Questions, continued

Questions for William Hughes, slave hunter and lawman

    1. What does slavery mean to you, Mr. Hughes?

    2. In your own words, what is an abolitionist?

    3. Why did Dr. Collins and Mr. Taylor hire you and send you to Boston with Mr. Knight?

    4. You defend the Fugitive Slave Law strongly. Why?

    Ask you own questions.

_____

_____

_____

_____

Questions for Frederick Douglass, former slave and abolitionist

    1. What was your childhood like?

    2. You were an educated slave. How did you learn to read and write?

    3. Why did you leave the United States in 1845 after writing your autobiography?

    4. How do you feel about the Fugitive Slave Law?

    Ask your own questions.

_____

_____

_____

_____

Diary Entry

Henry Clay

October, 1850

This presidency has been incredible! Taylor, a Mexican War hero, leads America during a period of enormous growth and prosperity. Lots of land, lots of people, and immigrants continuing to swarm into the country. Then gold is discovered in California, which ignites even more dreams. The railroads are expanding at a fast pace, the telegraph has improved communication tremendously, our foreign trade is wonderful, and even the invention of the sewing machine has improved our economic well-being.

The issue of slavery is the one force that dampens the American spirit. The more the North riots against its inhumane treatments, the more the South tries to declare it a national blessing. How else can they continue to produce so much cotton and bring us such wealth? I don't know what to do anymore. The two sides are growing angrier each day.

California wants to be admitted into the Union. The abolitionists are speaking out forcibly against slavery and acting upon it with riots. The slave states are demanding a fair share of the newly acquired land from the Mexican war, and if they don't get it, they will most assuredly seek secession from the Union.

All of a sudden we have to solve a serious problem, and it needs to be done quickly. A conflict is inevitable! We must stop these two sides from destroying everything we have worked so hard to establish.

"I conjure gentlemen, whether from the South or the North, by all they hold dear in this world, by all their love of liberty . . . by all the duties which they owe to mankind and all the duties they owe to themselves . . . I implore them to pause – solemnly to pause – at the edge of the precipice before the fearful and disastrous leap is taken in the yawning abyss below which will inevitably lead to certain and irretrievable destruction."

Our goal, the goal of the century, is to maintain our Union.

Ellen Craft

October, 1850

It's been almost three days since Reverend Parker brought me here to the Loring's home to hide. We had to go to the Reverend for help when Mr. Knight came to visit William at the cabinet shop. He spent a lot of time trying to get William to come out of the cabinet shop. Why would this white man want to see us? We never thought of him as one of our friends. We suspected that Mr. Knight was up to no good.

Sure enough, Reverend Parker told us that a jailer from Macon was with Mr. Knight. His name was Hughes. I remember him from Macon. He was a bully and made me feel real uncomfortable. He looked at me like I was dirty or something. He watched me carefully like he was going to make sure I didn't get away with anything because my skin was so white. While people who look at me may think I am white, I am really black, and I have learned to hate the color I wear on the outside.

William and I have been in Boston for over a year and a half. We've found good jobs, made money for ourselves, and have a fine house. We have found friends of our color to be with and learned to trust some white folks and call them friends, too. It took a long time to feel good about the white people, a long time. We have listened to William Lloyd Garrison, Lewis Hayden and Frederick Douglass, all black abolitionist leaders here in town. They helped us learn how to trust good white people.

These friends have helped William and me. They've been doing lots of things to show the government they don't like the Fugitive Slave Law. They are standing up against the government and the unjust laws. We are Americans. No one from Macon can come up here, tie us up and take us back there to be slaves again.

William Hughes

October 1850

John and I reached Boston this morning. We checked in at the United States Hotel, one of the finest in the town, knowing that Dr. Collins and Mr. Taylor would be paying the bill. We'll be staying here for a few days. Why not enjoy ourselves?

We're here to find William and Ellen Craft. John worked with William in Macon in the cabinet shop before he and his wife got the crazy idea to run off. Those slaves, don't they know they belong to someone who needs their help? How can they just pick up and leave and expect to live on their own? I bet these two runaways aren't even alive. I bet they're dead. They probably couldn't find food, work, or a place to stay. Who would want to hire them, anyway? They belong with the people who own them.

Maybe those abolitionists helped them. I've heard stories about them. There's even a story about a black lawyer who defends slaves in the courtroom. Ha! I'd like to see that! No slave I've ever seen was educated. They're not smart enough to learn, I guess. How could one of them be a lawyer?

The law will get those abolitionists, though. There are heavy fines and jail time for helping runaway slaves. We won't have any trouble. I even saw a poster up on the church across the street that stated, "Obey the Law - Do Not Partake in the Escape of Fugitive Slaves!" At least some people up here in the North believe in obeying the law.

We'll find those two fugitives. I can see myself now, riding into town with the two of them in the wagon. Dr. Collins and Mr. Taylor will pay me well when I bring these two in.

Diary Entry

Frederick Douglass

October, 1850

Faneuil Hall . . . 340 white abolitionists . . . hundreds of others, including slaves looking for abolitionist support in defying the Fugitive Slave Law.

Asked to speak, I rose to an ovation and said, "Boston Negroes have vowed to die rather than return to bondage. We must be prepared, should this law be put into operation, to see the streets of Boston running with blood."

I then asked the audience if they would permit slave holders to seize a Negro in Boston. Faneuil's guests sent out a resounding "no" that filled every rafter. "NO!" they shouted.

By the end of the meeting, two resolutions had been adopted. One was to work to repeal the Fugitive Slave Law, and the other stated that we would not allow a fugitive slave to be taken from Massachusetts regardless of what the constitution says.

A 55-member Committee of Vigilance was given an office and authority to provide advice and assistance to any fugitive slave needing help. This public meeting has done a lot to help our cause. We are all united, and we plan to defy this disgusting law until slavery has been erased from this country forever.

Ellen and William Craft have just informed us that they are being hunted by their previous owners. What luck! Here we are at the peak of our commitment and we are being given a chance to show our strength and unity for fugitive slaves. We will show these slave hunters just how strong we are here in Boston. They cannot come here and take away our citizens. Ellen and William Craft will NOT be taken from our city!

Fugitive Slave Law
What Really Happened

Monday morning, October 1850, brought a visitor to the cabinet shop. It was John Knight. Knight asked William to show him the town. William, feeling uneasy, told him he was too busy and couldn't leave the store. He knew he'd have to remain polite and calm. After all, he didn't want to bring any attention to the visitor, especially with the Fugitive Slave Law just having been passed.

Tuesday, Knight came to see William again. He wanted William to go for a walk. Again, William said he was too busy to leave the shop. Knight then asked him to bring Ellen to his hotel that evening. Ellen and William did not go, of course. They prayed for their safety.

On Wednesday they received a note from Knight to bring any messages for their families and friends in Georgia to the hotel that night for he would be returning to Macon the next day. William and Ellen got nervous. Knight probably came with a slave catcher. Would they come kidnap them in their home while they slept?

William and Ellen went to Reverend Parker's house to tell him what had been happening. He took Ellen to a home outside of town for hiding and made sure William was armed before letting him go home. William would have to stay there so as not to alarm too many people. Reverend Parker alerted the Vigilance Committee made up of several respected abolitionists (Hayden, Garrison, Douglass, Sumner, and Phillips).

William stayed in his home through Sunday, not closing an eye once. Exhausted and mentally anguished over the possibility that Ellen had been taken, he made his way to the Lansing home where Ellen had been hiding. The neighborhood heard of their flight, thus prompting them to seek refuge somewhere more safe. Ellen hid in Reverend Parker's home, while William stayed in Hayden's home.

William watched as Hayden and others printed posters warning of the two slave hunters, Knight and Hughes. Vigilance Committee members followed the two all around town, since they did not leave as they had said they would, jeering them and saying, "Go back to Georgia, you slave hunters!"

During this time, the abolitionist lawyers formed a Legal Committee that issued a warrant for the arrest of Hughes. They charged him with conspiracy to kidnap and with slandering William's name (he had boasted that William had been a thief, taking his master's clothes, which he had not), Hughes was arraigned in court and bail was set at $10,000. The bail was paid by a wealthy Boston merchant who agreed to aid the anti-abolitionists, and Hughes was freed. The courtroom was full of angry abolitionists, determined to oppose the Fugitive Slave Law. Knight escaped back to the hotel, and Hughes was almost shot by an irate Bostonian.

The Reverend Parker, content that justice was taking its course, sought to have Hughes and Knight leave town as soon as possible before someone was hurt. He said, "I have heard that Hughes is going to leave Boston tomorrow morning. We will see to it that he does."

At six o'clock the next morning, Parker and about 20 other Committee members went to the hotel to see Hughes. Thinking he would escape, they positioned themselves at all of the hotel's exits.

Hughes finally emerged. Nervous and completely agitated at the sight of the crowd, he said to Parker, "But we came here to execute the law!"

Parker told him they would never be able to safely take the Crafts out of Boston, and reluctantly Hughes agreed to leave. Parker encouraged them to get on the train quickly because he could not promise complete safety anymore.

The two, worried that something would happen to them if they boarded the train in Boston, fled to Newton Corner and boarded the train there.

Ellen and William were not safe in Boston, though. Anyone could come and capture them and claim the reward. They would have to leave. They left Boston to board a ship for England. There, William found a good job, and life became more peaceful. They were even able to have a family of their own, all English-born, but free. They would return someday, after the Civil War, but only to relive the tensions of being black. The war had not left a completely equal and free society for blacks in America.

Hughes and Knight were last seen in New York, disgruntled and completely baffled by the entire experience in Boston. Did they ever return home to Macon? No one knows for sure.

Clay, the Great Compromiser, died in 1852, feeling overwhelmed with the reality of troubles between the American people. His compromise of 1850, although temporarily halting the states' disunion, would not save the destruction of the Union that lay ahead. North and South, Union and Confederacy, blue and gray, would eventually clash. Not yet 100 years old, the United States would be torn apart by the Civil War.